Effective Teachers, Effective Schools

Second-Language Teaching in Australia,
Canada, England and the United States

MARY ASHWORTH

Pippin

Designed by John Zehethofer
Edited by Dyanne Rivers
Printed and bound in Canada by Friesens

We acknowledge the financial support of the Government
of Canada through the Book Publishing Industry Development
Program for our publishing activities.

Canadian Cataloguing in Publication Data

Ashworth, Mary
   Effective teachers, effective schools: second-language teaching
in Australia, Canada, England and the United States

Includes bibliographical references.
ISBN 0-88751-089-2

1. English language — Study and teaching as a second language
(Elementary).* 2. English language — Study and teaching as a
second language (Secondary).*
I. Title.

PE1128.A2A745 1999   428'.0071   C99-931559-5

ISBN 0-88751-089-2

10   9   8   7   6   5   4   3   2   1

For Cecily Brash

ACKNOWLEDGMENTS

I would like to thank the many people and institutions who responded so willingly and quickly to my requests for information about English-as-a-second-language education for children and adolescents—and for their offers of further help if I should need it.

Special thanks to my colleague, Dr. Bernard Mohan, for his help and support over many years.

I would also like to acknowledge Richard Kidd and Brenda Marquardson for helping me come to a full understanding of the Foresee approach.

In addition, the following people contributed to this book in a variety of ways and deserve honourable mention:

Carol Chandler, Elizabeth Coelho, Maggie Cooper, Mary G. Curtis, Catherine Eddy, Carole Edwards, Charlotte Franson, Jean Handscombe, Lynne Hannigan, Sylvia Helmer, Constant Leung, Gerry Morisseau, Glenda J. Redden, Lia Ridley, Penthes Rubrecht, Virginia L. Sauvé, Hugh South, Maggie Warbey and my editor, Dyanne Rivers.

CONTENTS

EFFECTIVE TEACHERS, EFFECTIVE SCHOOLS

. . . .

INTRODUCTION

W hen I started teaching on the West Side of Vancouver, British Columbia, in the mid-1950s, 10-year-old Sue Wong was the only child in the school whose first language was not English. Sue's spoken English was almost incomprehensible and she had great difficulty with both reading and writing. As a result, like many others before and after her, she had been labelled a slow learner. During a parent-teacher interview, I asked Sue's mother what language the family spoke at home. In very broken English, she told me that they always spoke English. "Alway," she asserted firmly.

At the time, I had never heard of English as a second language, and it was only later that I realized that Sue was an ESL student. Still, my instinct told me that this child would have been better off speaking good Cantonese—rather than poor English—at home.

That encounter with Sue marked the beginning of my journey into the world of English as a second language. It's a world that has changed dramatically since I first stepped into it. If Sue were attending her school today, she would no longer be the odd one out—80 per cent of the students now speak English as a second language! And for those who need help in learning this second language, there is plenty of support.

For years, I was happily employed training English-as-a-second-language teachers for schools or adult programs, as well as researching, writing and speaking in the field. With retirement came time to travel, time I used to talk to educators in Australia, Canada, England and the United States about what they are doing for non-English-speaking immigrant children. What they told me, what I saw going on in classrooms, and what I gleaned from nearly 800 documents—policy statements, laws, handbooks, guidelines, brochures, newsletters and so on—sent to me by ESL administrators, consultants and teachers in all four countries inspired this book.

Those of us who have been in education for any length of time know that research and practice lead to new developments in the ways children are educated. We also know that knowledge of these developments does not always filter through to those who could use it most—administrators and classroom teachers. As a result, I decided to create a forum for the sharing of ideas about many of the good things that are going on in Australia, Canada, England and the United States.

The book begins, though, by taking a step back to review immigration patterns and the history of English as a second language in the four countries. The reason for this is straightforward: an understanding of the past helps us avoid repeating the mistakes of the past, while enabling us to hang on to practices that work. As T.S. Eliot wrote in *Four Quartets:* "Burnt Norton":

Time present and time past
Are both perhaps present in time future,
And time future contained in time past.

From this beginning, the book moves on to its main focus: a survey of what is happening right now in second-language education in the four countries. Policies, students, teachers, programs, bilingual education, teaching methods, and parents and communities are examined.

When embarking on this project, I made a decision to write in the very personal first person. I want to explain what I think in the hope that you will agree or disagree with my views—and that your reaction to my words will inspire you to take action. There is no standing still in education; there is only going backwards or forwards. We have come a long way in providing quality education for non-English-speaking immigrant children, but the journey—theirs and yours—is not over yet.

Some of the important issues that are likely to face ESL children and their teachers in the future are outlined in the final chapter, titled "Looking Ahead." This chapter is short because I cannot predict with any certainty what will happen down the road. It is you, after all, who will pick up the torch for future generations of second-language students. What I can do, however, is pose questions and present options that I hope will help you exert a positive influence on the quality of education provided to the non-English-speaking children in your care.

In writing the book, I chose to exclude options that represent, in my opinion, poor teaching practice. Though I have occasionally included a negative comment to highlight what I believe teachers should be doing, I have not acknowledged practices whose only merit is to illustrate what should *not* be done. After all, these practices may have changed for the better since the day I first came across them and, as far as possible, I want to highlight features that I consider educationally sound.

As I compiled the material, it quickly became apparent that the terms used to describe students whose first language is not English vary considerably among the four countries. In Australia, these students are known as non-English-speaking-background—NESB—students; in Canada, they are called English-as-a-second-language—ESL—students; in England, they are bilingual students; and in the United States, they are limited-English-proficient—LEP—students or bilingual students.

The term "bilingual" may confuse some Canadian readers, who are used to hearing it used in a very specific context. Canada has two official languages: English and French. Someone who is bilingual can speak both. For more than three decades, English-speaking children in Canada have had the option of taking their elementary and high school education in both French and English. As a result, a bilingual student is usually someone who is being educated in both English and French. There are, of course, many children in Canada who speak English or French *and* another language; when this is the case, it is usual to specify what the other language is. In the United States, on the other hand, the term refers to a student who is enrolled in a program that uses both English and the child's first language.

For the sake of brevity, to avoid confusion, and because it is most familiar to me, I have chosen to use the term "English as a second language" or "ESL" when referring to students whose first language is not English—unless I am quoting directly from documents produced in jurisdictions where a different term prevails. When this is the case, the language of the document is used.

The terms used to describe a child's first language also vary among the countries. It may be called the home language, heritage language, community language, L1, mother tongue, and even other Australian languages. I have chosen to use "first language" unless a different term is used in quotations drawn directly from the documents produced in the various jurisdictions.

To help keep these terms and others straight, a list of abbreviations is provided on page 145.

Two other sections are also found at the end of the book. The section titled "Contributors" lists the jurisdictions that supplied material or welcomed me as a visitor—or did both. "References and Resources" is a chapter-by-chapter list of references, which introduces the people and institutions in all four countries who are engaging in activities that I think are good for ESL. You may wish to add some of their names to your network of ESL sources.

Now I invite you to join me on my journey through the world of ESL as I have found it in Australia, Canada, England and the United States. Our journey begins on the following page with Neil Horne's poem, "I Am an ESL Student." As associate superintendent in the Vancouver School District, British Columbia, Horne was responsible for, among other things, the education of ESL students. Through the eyes of an ESL student, his poem looks at the culture the student hopes to become a part of.

I Am an ESL Student

I am an ESL student
...I did not choose to be here, or to leave my friends, or to
  leave my home
...I do not look like my brother or my sister; I look like me
  and that is normal; it is you who looks strange
...I am very fortunate because at the end of the day I will
  have two or three languages
...you see, I am an ESL student...
...I like blue jeans—the first time I saw my national dress
  was at a multicultural night at my new Canadian school
...I do not live on strange ethnic foods; I like ice cream,
  pizza, Coca-Cola and junk food
...I am not by birthright a mathematics or science scholar
...you see, I am an ESL student...
...I am a child en route to adulthood and that trip will be as
  challenging for me as for any other young person
...I am not by ethnic definition a gang member, a cheat, a
  male chauvinist, a suppressed female, a bad driver, a
  compulsive gambler, or part of a close-knit extended
  family
...I am not learning disabled, educationally retarded or in
  need of fixing; I just don't speak, write or read English
  well, but that will change
... you see, I am an ESL student ...
...I am as unique as any Canadian-born young person and,
  as a group, my friends and I are as different and as
  similar as any group of young people
...I would prefer to attend my neighbourhood school and to
  become part of my community
...I have parents who are very involved in my education;
  they may not, however, share your definition of
  involvement
...you see, I am an ESL student ...
...I, like you, have a personality that has been shaped, in
  part, by my culture; my parents, like your parents, have
  personalities shaped by their cultures; therefore, we are
  different, and therefore, both of us must remember that
  our personalities are neither good nor bad—they are just
  what they are

...I come from a culture that is not without racist aspects; I
   have as much to learn about living in harmony as you do
...you see, I am an ESL student...
...I have a need to love and be loved, to praise and be
   praised, to correct and be corrected
...you see, I am an ESL student

Neil Horne

. . . . 1

HISTORY, LAWS AND POLICIES

The world's history is interwoven with migrations. The poor and
the persecuted have left their homeland for other countries. The
great movement of peoples from eastern to western Europe and farther west across the Atlantic to the United States, Canada, the Ar-
gentine, Australasia and South Africa continued throughout the
19th century, most of the emigrants being unskilled workers from
rural areas.

A History of the World in the Twentieth Century
J.A.S. Grenville

Three kinds of immigrants continue to seek new
lives in Canada, Australia, England and the United States.
Some are economic immigrants—people seeking jobs; others
are refugees—people seeking to escape political or religious
persecution; and still others are family members—people
seeking to join relatives who have preceded them. Countries
welcome these immigrants when their work skills are needed,
but are often less receptive during depressions and periods of
high unemployment.

Over two or three centuries, Canada, Australia and the
United States have taken in millions of immigrants who have
helped build these countries by moving into the vast open
spaces occupied by Aboriginal peoples. England's experience
with immigrants on a similar scale is, however, a more recent
phenomenon.

In the rapidly growing post-World War II economies of all
four countries, there was not enough labour to meet the needs
of business and industry. As a result, these countries usually
welcomed immigrants, who arrived, often with their families,
in ever-increasing numbers. For Canada, Australia and the
United States, coping with immigrant children who did not
speak English and whose cultural backgrounds were very different from those of native-born citizens was nothing new. All
three countries had experienced previous waves of immigra-

tion, though never in such numbers. For England, however, the influx of immigrants presented a new challenge.

I was one of those post-war immigrants to Canada. I left England for Canada in 1949, intending to see a bit of the world before returning home to settle down. I spent a few months in Toronto, then travelled by train across the vast Canadian Prairies to Vancouver. Once there, it took me only a few weeks to decide that this was where I wanted to live for the rest of my life. In 1954, I switched careers, abandoning stenography in favour of teaching. In 1955—my first year in a classroom—I met Sue Wong and began my journey into English as a second language.

As my experience with ESL broadened, I began examining the history of Canada, particularly its immigration laws, which governed who was welcome and who was not. I was interested in how these laws affected—and continued to affect—ESL teaching. Then, as the idea for this book took shape, I began studying immigration patterns in Australia, England and the United States for the same reason.

Canada
Population: 30 million

Before the coming of the Europeans, Canada was populated by Aboriginal peoples. Quebec, Ontario and the Atlantic provinces were settled first by European fur traders, fishers, and farmers, as well as Black slaves seeking their freedom. The Prairies became home to religious groups—Hutterites, Mennonites and Doukhobors—and to national groups—Ukrainians, Germans and Scandinavians. As the 20th century dawned west of the Rocky Mountains, the predominantly British population there became gravely concerned about the number of Asians—Chinese, Japanese and Southeast Asians—entering the province. In 1913, more than 400,000 newcomers entered Canada, then a country of only seven million people.

In the early 1920s, immigration from Asia was banned. Nevertheless, the number of Chinese, Southeast Asian and, particularly, Japanese children in the schools steadily increased. Single Japanese men who had immigrated before the ban came into effect often married by proxy, choosing their wives from photographs sent by relatives in Japan. These "picture brides" were permitted to enter Canada. After the bombing of Pearl Harbor in 1941, the country was gripped by fear that people of Japanese descent would side with Japan if Canada were invaded. This fear was especially strong in B.C., where Japanese immigrants had settled in large numbers. As a result, Canadian-born children of Japanese descent, along with their mothers, were moved away from the West Coast to inland camps. Their fathers and older brothers were sent to work on farms east of the Rockies. Their land and possessions were confiscated and sold at bargain prices, ostensibly to pay for their stay in the camps. In fact, all were loyal Canadian citizens. In 1988, the Canadian government finally apologized for this unfair treatment, and promised that nothing like this would occur again.

Although immigration had slowed to a trickle during World War I and the Great Depression of the 1930s, the Canadian economy boomed for many years after World War II and immigrants were welcomed, especially if they were white. In 1945, the British Columbia Elections Act had awarded to Asians who had served in the military in World War I or II the right to vote in provincial elections. Previously, Asians had been barred from voting. Two years later, the Canadian Citizenship Act defined the franchise as a right of citizenship, and B.C. amended its provincial legislation accordingly. This change meant that citizens of Asian descent were finally able to vote alongside all other Canadians.

On May 1, 1947, the government of William Lyon Mackenzie King repealed the 1923 Chinese Immigration Act, which had barred Chinese people from entering Canada and prevented those already living here from voting. In his statement to the House of Commons announcing the repeal, King set out a series of principles designed to govern future immigration to Canada:

— Immigration must both increase the size of the population and improve the standard of living by fostering economic growth.
— Immigration must be selective and related to the ability of Canada to absorb the newcomers.
— Immigration must be considered a privilege, not a right.

Because King and his government believed that the people of Canada did not wish to alter the fundamental character of the population, the repeal did not lift all restrictions on Asian immigration. Only Chinese people who were Canadian citizens, for example, had the right to bring their families to Canada. By the mid-1950s, though, the government had relaxed some of the regulations that had placed prospective immigrants from countries outside Europe at a disadvantage. Further changes to the Immigration Act in 1962 and 1967 established a points system for applicants. Those whose education or training filled a need in the Canadian workforce, as well as those who spoke English or French, for example, were awarded more points. This made it easier for people of colour, refugees and people from developing countries to gain entry.

New Canadian children, as they were then called, began to take their seats alongside native-born students in classrooms across the country, especially in areas where the skills of family members were in high demand. At the same time, in response to changing labour markets, some French-speaking Canadians were also migrating to new homes elsewhere in the country, where their children began attending English-speaking schools. Because describing the French-speaking children of Canadian citizens as new Canadians was considered inappropriate, all non-English-speaking children in English-speaking schools came to be described as students of English as a second language.

French is the first language of many Canadians. Yet, for years, French shared official-language status with English in only two provinces: Quebec and Manitoba. Then, in 1969, the Royal Commission on Bilingualism and Biculturalism issued a report that laid the groundwork for passage of the Official Languages Act. This act gave French and English equal status as the languages of the federal administration. The Commission's report also suggested that bilingualism—the ability to speak English and French—and multiculturalism, a term that has become widely used to mean cultural pluralism, might complement each other.

Two years later, Prime Minister Pierre Trudeau announced that "multiculturalism in a bilingual framework" would become the foundation of government policy. Following this lead, some provincial governments also formulated policies on multiculturalism and racism.

In 1978, a new federal immigration act revised the basic principles underlying immigration policy, giving expression to concern for the individual as well as for the nation. The new legislation set out Canada's social, economic, demographic and cultural goals, banned discrimination, encouraged family reunion, and promoted humanitarian concern for refugees. It also required all levels of government to work in co-operation with volunteer organizations to help immigrants adapt to Canadian society.

In 1982, the Charter of Rights and Freedoms, which outlaws discrimination, was enshrined in the Canadian Constitution. The Canadian Multiculturalism Act of 1988 strengthened the government's commitment to multiculturalism and set out the principles that would govern the country's cultural policies:

— To recognize and promote an understanding that multiculturalism reflects the cultural and racial diversity of Canadian society.
— To ensure that all individuals receive equal treatment and equal protection under the law.

Today, between 190,000 and 215,000 immigrants arrive in Canada every year. They may be independent immigrants, refugees or members of families that are already in Canada.

GOVERNMENT POLICY AND ESL PROGRAMS

In response to the federal government's policy of promoting multiculturalism, some provinces incorporated into their school systems programs designed to encourage children to continue speaking their first language. In other provinces, first-language classes, usually organized by ethnic associations, were held after school or on Saturdays.

Little by little, as the cultural and linguistic needs of non-English-speaking children came to be recognized, English-as-a-second-language programs were also established. At first, most of these were in large cities, where most newcomers tended to settle. Because the education of children is a provincial responsibility in Canada, no federal funding is available for ESL programs. All ESL programs are funded by provincial governments and school districts. In an attempt to encourage bilingualism, however, federal money is available for teaching French to English-speaking children. This has led to a curious anomaly: a school in Vancouver, for example, may receive federal funding to teach French to a Cantonese-speaking immigrant child, but federal money is not available to teach the same child English, the medium of instruction in most British Columbia schools.

During the past two or three decades, various provincial governments have set up royal commissions to formulate recommendations for improving the school system in their jurisdiction. Too often, however, these commissions have paid scant attention to ESL education; nonetheless, some provinces have adopted policies that have not only increased the number and variety of ESL classes, but also improved teacher-training courses in ESL.

Australia
Population: 18 million

For at least 40,000 years before the first Europeans arrived, Aborigines and Torres Strait Islanders lived on the continent of Australia. Until the American Revolution, British criminals sentenced to deportation had been shipped to the southern colonies of what was to become the United States of America. There, they had been sold to planters as workers. Because the American Revolution cut short this practice, the British government had to find a new place to dump its convicts. In 1786, Lord Sydney, a minister in William Pitt's government in London, instructed the Admiralty to prepare enough ships to take convicts to Botany Bay, Australia. On May 13, 1787, the first ships—filled with thieves, dissolute characters, prostitutes and others—set out, reaching their destination by mid-January 1788. The practice of transporting British convicts to Australia continued into the late 1860s, when public opinion brought it to a stop.

Convicts were not, however, the only Europeans to arrive in Australia. After their tour of duty in the Southern Hemisphere was over, for example, some army officers stayed to try their hand at farming. Irish Catholics also came, along with their priests, as did some Europeans from other countries, and some Asians.

For nearly a century after 1860, public opinion generally favoured excluding non-whites from Australia, a feeling that was reflected in the country's immigration policies. In 1901, for example, the Immigration Restriction Bill enabled officials to rule that anyone who failed to pass a dictation test of 50 words in a European language was a prohibited immigrant. In 1905, students, tourists and businesspeople from India and Japan were permitted to enter the country, but their stay was limited to five years. In 1912, the same concession was granted to Chinese people.

During World War I, Australians served in the military alongside British, Canadian and American men and women. When the war was over, William Morris Hughes rose in the House of Representatives to remind members that they had entered the conflict to defend their national integrity, to safeguard their liberties and their free institutions of government, and "...to maintain those ideals which we have nailed to the very topmost of our flagpoles—White Australia, and those other aspirations of this young Democracy."

On September 3, 1939, a second world war, even more terrible than the first, began when Hitler invaded Poland. When the guns of Europe and Asia were finally silenced in 1945, Australians feared that Asians might start immigrating in large numbers. As a result, the government made plans to fill the country's empty spaces with Europeans, particularly the British, and introduced immigration policies to encourage this. For example, some British citizens who had served in the armed forces during the war—and members of their families—were offered free passage to Australia; others paid a nominal sum of £10.

By the late 1960s, however, public opinion was starting to change and the White Australia policy was liberalized, resulting in an influx of refugees from Asia and Eastern Europe. In 1939, 98 per cent of Australians had either been born in the British Isles or were descended from British families. Forty years later, the post-war influx of refugees from the Baltic States, Russia, Poland, the two Germanies, Holland, Yugoslavia, Greece, Italy and Turkey had changed the makeup of Australia so that more than 11 per cent of the population had no connection with the British Isles.

As Australians embraced multiculturalism and more children from non-English-speaking backgrounds took their places in Australian schools that had developed from the British model, it became apparent that measures were needed to accommodate the cultural and linguistic needs of the new arrivals. For example, until the Immigration (Education) Act was passed in 1971, there had been no special provision or funding for teaching ESL to immigrant children in Australia. Passage of this act cleared the way for introducing the Child Migrant Education Program. In South Australia, this program provided for the hiring of 20 teachers, who were assigned to schools with a high population of ESL children. In 1975, the special needs of new arrivals were officially recognized by the federal government and special funding was provided for refugees. In 1976, the Commonwealth Schools Commission assumed responsibility for CMEP.

The National Agenda for a Multicultural Australia (1989), the National Goals for Schooling in Australia (1989) and the Australian Language and Literacy Policy (1991) delineated some of the key priorities for promoting multiculturalism in education, such as encouraging cultural awareness and the retention of first languages.

The National Equity Program for Schools was introduced in 1991 to ensure that all students have equal access to quality education. The program set out policies in four areas: access, equity, national priorities and incentives. The access element supplies funding for both the New Arrivals Program, which helps provide intensive ESL instruction to newly arrived students, and the General Support Program, which continues to help ESL students after they move on to mainstream classrooms. The equity element addresses the needs of disadvantaged schools, such as inner-city schools, while the national priorities element includes policies for dealing with both students at risk of failing to learn and those who are gifted or talented. The incentives element deals with gender equity and students with disabilities.

Although the needs of ESL students are specifically addressed in only the access element, which includes an ESL component, the document acknowledged that non-English-speaking children, like their English-speaking counterparts, are found throughout the school population and are, therefore, affected by policies in all four areas. Some ESL students, for example, attend inner-city schools, which are included in the equity element; others are gifted or talented; and still others have disabilities.

In 1994, *ESL Scales* was published. According to its foreword, the document represented "the most significant collaborative curriculum development project in the history of Australian education." Designed to help improve teaching and learning and to provide a common language for reporting students' achievement, *ESL Scales* identified eight learning areas—the arts, health and physical education, mathematics, society and environment, English, languages other than English, and science and technology. Each learning area was organized into strands, representing its content, process and concepts. Each was also organized into bands, representing the stages at which knowledge, understanding and skills in the area are developed. *ESL Scales* provided benchmarks for measuring the achievement of ESL learners and developed a shared language that could be used by teachers of ESL students.

In addition to this national initiative, individual states have introduced their own programs. For example, in 1991, a program called Multicultural Education Initiatives 1990-1992 began addressing the need to provide a policy for multicultural education in New South Wales. From this grew the Multicultural Education Plan for 1993-1997 and the Ethnic Affairs Policy Statement Plan for 1993-1997, which set out "management practices that will promote access to all the department's educational services, and the full participation of students and staff from diverse cultural and linguistic backgrounds." South Australia enacted its Equal Opportunity Act in 1984, and Western Australia introduced its Social Justice in Education Policy in 1991. In 1994, the Queensland Department of Education published its Social Justice Strategy for 1994-1998, which committed it to helping all students achieve quality educational outcomes. A section of the document specifically addressed the needs of students from diverse cultural and linguistic backgrounds.

South Australia prepared a Settlement Plan 1993-1997, which dealt with settlement, income support, housing and accommodation, as well as education and children's services.

The state of Victoria completed some research into ESL in government schools in 1992 and later published a curriculum and standards framework in eight key learning areas to help schools provide for the English-language learning needs of ESL students.

These are far from the only initiatives introduced in Australia, a country that has produced more policies, programs and practices than I have space to recount!

United States
Population: 273 million

During most of the 19th century, settlers in the United States usually came from Europe. They often arrived in search of cheap farmland, which was no longer available in their homeland, though some, like the Irish, sought relief from poverty and political persecution. In 1907, 1,285,000 immigrants arrived in the land where, it was said, dreams came true. But as early as the mid-19th century, language was a source of conflict between those who did and those who did not speak English.

In the 20th century, immigration from China and Japan was stopped well before the beginning of World War I, and even immigration from Europe was cut back for a time after 1924. The Great Depression of the 1930s and World War II extended the period of relatively low immigration. When the fighting stopped, however, the economy was on the upswing and the government once more opened the gates to immigration.

More than 11 million people entered the U.S. between 1941 and 1980. Puerto Ricans and Filipinos, members of the U.S. empire, had the right to enter and came by the thousands. Mexicans crossed the southern border to California, some legally and some illegally, to find jobs in the growing economy of that state. Wars in Asia brought an influx from Taiwan, Korea and Vietnam. Cubans crossed the water in flimsy craft and landed on the shores of Florida. As a result of the specific migration patterns of people from various cultural groups, the population of some states is more mixed than that of others. In New Mexico, for example, eight languages and cultures have co-existed since the early Spanish settlers started arriving in 1598.

Some states or school districts set up programs to cope with the new arrivals. New York State, for example, established a Bilingual Education Unit in 1969. On the other side of the continent, the Seattle School District established an ESL program in 1970. At the time, it served about 100 students with three teachers and three interns. In 1982, Rhode Island enacted the English Language Proficiency Act, which required all school districts in the state to provide programs and services to ensure that ESL students have the same educational opportunities as their native English-speaking peers. Though most states have now mandated programs to accommodate ESL students, a few—usually those where the population of non-English-speaking children is small—still have no set policies for school districts to follow. In response to my request for information, an official of one of these states wrote: "Essentially, schools are guided by the policies set forth by the Office for Civil Rights."

Policies for teaching English as a second language to children have been influenced by federal and state laws and by court cases, many of which established precedents. A key piece of legislation, which laid the foundation for both introducing laws and launching legal challenges to established practices, was the 1964 Civil Rights Act. It stated, "No person in the United States shall, on the ground of race, colour, or national origin ... be denied the benefits of, or be subjected to discrimination under any program or activity receiving Federal financial assistance."

The federal Bilingual Education Act was enacted on January 1, 1968. Known as Title VII, its initial purpose was to provide federal funding for establishing bilingual education programs in which ESL students are taught in both their first language and English. Funds were provided to every state for teacher training and research, as well as for instructional programs. In 1970, a memorandum from the federal Department of Health, Education and Welfare interpreted the 1964 Civil Rights Act as follows:

— Where inability to speak and understand the English language excludes national origin minority group children from effective participation in the educational program offered by a school district, the district must take affirmative steps to rectify the language deficiency in order to open its instructional program to these students.

— School districts must not assign national origin minority group students to classes for the mentally retarded on the basis of criteria which essentially measure or evaluate English-language skills; nor may school districts deny national origin minority group children access to college preparatory courses on a basis directly related to the failure of the school system to inculcate English-language skills.

— Any ability grouping or tracking system employed by the school system to deal with the special language skill needs of national origin minority group children must be designed to meet such language skill needs as soon as possible and must not operate as an educational dead end or permanent track.

— School districts must adequately notify national origin minority group parents of school activities which are called to the attention of other parents. Such notice in order to be adequate may have to be provided in a language other than English.

The Equal Educational Opportunities Act of 1974, declared: "No state shall deny equal educational opportunity to an individual on account of his or her race, colour, sex or national origin, by…the failure of an educational agency to take appropriate action to overcome language barriers that impede participation by its students in its instructional programs."

This legislation was the direct result of a class-action lawsuit filed by 13 non-English-speaking students, seven of whom had been born in the United States, on behalf of nearly 3,000 Chinese-speaking students in the San Francisco Unified School District. The suit charged that these students had been denied the right to an education because they could not function in English, the language of the school; as a result, they were doomed to become dropouts and to suffer prolonged unemployment.

The case went to the U.S. Supreme Court, which handed down its judgment on January 21, 1974. The court ruled that the failure of the school district to provide English-language instruction to non-English-speaking children denied them the right to participate in the educational program, and therefore violated their right to equal educational opportunity as guaranteed by the U.S. Constitution and the state of California. The court ruled that simply providing the same facilities, textbooks, teachers and curriculum to students who do not understand English does not constitute equal treatment. Furthermore, the court pointed out that basic English skills are at the core of what schools teach. As a result, requiring children to acquire these skills *before* they can begin to effectively participate in educational programs "is to make a mockery of public education."

Ten years later, an amendment to the Bilingual Education Act described ESL students as a national resource and allocated funds for six types of instructional program—transitional bilingual education, developmental bilingual education, special alternative English instruction, programs of academic excellence, family English literacy programs, and programs for gifted or talented students.

To bolster national statutes banning discrimination, some states passed their own laws. In 1971, for example, Massachusetts specified that everyone has the right to attend public schools in the town where he or she lives. Massachusetts also became the first state to pass a bilingual education law. In 1990, Maine amended its Human Rights Act to give all children and adults the right to freedom from discrimination in education because of sex, a physical or mental handicap, or national origin.

In the 1970s and '80s, decisions on three separate cases heard in federal courts established important precedents that affected the education of immigrant children. One required a municipal school district to design an educational plan to address the needs of non-English-speaking students by implementing a bilingual and bicultural curriculum, revising testing procedures, and recruiting and hiring bilingual school personnel. Another imposed a requirement that ESL and bilingual programs be properly evaluated. A third allowed immigrant children to attend school, even when their immigration documents did not conform to official requirements.

In 1990, President George Bush announced a series of educational goals and set the year 2000 as the deadline for achieving them. While the stated goals are certainly worth working toward, the possibility of achieving them in a single decade was remote at best. For example, ensuring that all children in

America would start school ready to learn would have meant eradicating poverty and child abuse and educating some parents about the importance of working with their children in areas such as talking and reading. Furthermore, if the parents did not speak English, pre-school programs that could introduce ESL children to English and to the culture of the school would have been necessary. The goals also called for science, math, history, geography and English to be emphasized so that "all students learn to use their minds well, so they may be prepared for responsible citizenship, further learning, and productive employment in our modern economy." Again, this goal, though laudable, could not be achieved in the specified time frame.

These were not the only extravagant items on the list. One goal, for example, called on U.S. students to be the first in the world in science and math achievement. Another stated that every adult American would be literate. Still another said that every school in the United States would be free of drugs and violence. With respect to achieving this last goal in particular, 1998 and 1999 were not good years: in fact, they were marked by some very violent acts in which teachers and students were killed by gunfire.

As the millennium approached, a backlash began to develop against bilingual programs. This was felt most strongly in California, where voters approved legislation restricting the availability of these programs. The impact of this legislation—and other initiatives that may curtail bilingual programs—is discussed in more detail in Chapter 6.

England
Population: 58 million

As in Canada, Australia and the United States, immigrants to England have been welcomed when their labour was needed. Until the second half of the 20th century, however, immigrants had not arrived in numbers large enough to affect the British culture or way of life.

This changed after World War II, however, when the government began actively recruiting immigrants to fill the need for both skilled and unskilled labour. An agreement between the United Kingdom and Italy, for example, brought thousands of Italian immigrants, so that the size of the Italian population is now about 200,000.

The U.K. also encouraged immigration from many other countries and had issued British passports to people born in its colonies. This led to waves of immigration from the West Indies, Hong Kong, India, Pakistan, Cyprus and Malta. At the time, schools promoted British traditions, history, customs and culture and, once immigrant children learned to speak English, it was assumed that they would be assimilated into the dominant culture. In the 1970s, however, ethnic parents who wanted their children to retain their first language and culture began to question the assimilation model. Gradually, the philosophy began to shift toward integration, and immigrants were no longer expected to abandon their own language and culture.

GOVERNMENT POLICY AND ESL PROGRAMS

In 1963, the British government decreed that immigrant children should make up no more than 30 per cent of a school's population. In some cases, this meant busing immigrant children to schools outside their neighbourhood. In addition, centres for ESL children were opened in many districts. As the years passed, both these practices came to be viewed as racist and misdirected, although busing continued in one area until 1979.

By the 1980s, various school jurisdictions were seeking ways of preparing all children, not just newcomers, for life in what had obviously become a multilingual, multicultural country. In 1975, the ground-breaking Bullock Report had recommended that school language policies be cross-curricular and that language education be considered the responsibility of every teacher.

Ten years later, the Swann Report, titled *Education for All*, called for an appreciation of the United Kingdom's growing diversity: "In our view 'Education for all' should involve more than learning about the cultures and lifestyles of various ethnic groups; it should also seek to develop in all pupils, both ethnic majority and minority, a flexibility of mind and an ability to analyze critically and rationally the nature of British society today within a global context. The reality of British society, now and in the future, is that a variety of ethnic groups, with their own distinct lifestyles and value systems, will be living together." The findings of both these reports influenced the 1986 Education Act and the 1988 Education Reform Act.

When the government began talking of introducing a national curriculum in the early 1990s, it sparked considerable debate among teachers of non-English-speaking immigrant children. Though most agreed that ESL students learn more effectively when integrated into classes with English-speaking children, they expressed concern about whether provision would be made for meeting the special needs of ESL students in a mainstream setting, especially when funding cuts were impending. To ensure that their concerns were taken into account, teachers and project leaders formed the National Association for Language Development in the Curriculum. In addition to giving ESL teachers a voice and enabling them to exchange views, NALDIC provided a forum for debating the wisdom of introducing a national curriculum, discussing its effects on ESL students, and initiating strategies for offsetting its adverse effects.

Since 1966, local education authorities have been able to request government funding for a portion of the salaries of ESL teachers, but the grants were available only to educate children born in countries that were members of the British Commonwealth. This situation existed until 1993, when the grants were extended to educate all non-English-speaking children.

In the United Kingdom, the concept of multicultural education remains the subject of debate. Some people contend, for example, that it places too much emphasis on culture, which may lead to a subtle form of racism and ethnic stereotyping.

. . . . 2

THE EVOLUTION OF POLICIES

Given the importance of language in our society, a language policy is essential. The policy must be based on a vision of the province which recognizes our traditions of the past and our multicultural heritage and diversity, but at the same time focuses on preparing young (people) for the future.

Language Education Policy for Alberta
Alberta Education

When I was training ESL teachers in the 1970s and '80s, I often used this maxim: There is nothing so practical as a good theory. Over the years, I have also come to believe that there is nothing so practical as a good policy. When I first entered the field, however, there was often not even a bad policy, let alone a good one, to govern ESL activities in British Columbia. In the early 1970s, Patricia Wakefield and I put together some ideas about ESL programs and the students who should qualify for them. In 1978, the British Columbia Ministry of Education published these, identifying them in the title of the document as "guidelines" and "suggestions"; in fact, it was to be another three years before the Ministry gathered its courage and published a policy. This is a story that has been repeated in other Canadian provinces, as well as in Australia, England and the United States.

Fortunately, times have changed since then and the educational authorities who control the destinies of the ESL children in their jurisdictions have, in most cases, established policies in a variety of areas. Before examining these, however, it's worth taking a look at who creates the policies that affect ESL children, teachers, administrators and parents.

How Policies Are Created

Policies affecting the teaching and learning of English as a second language may be created by bureaucrats who are far removed from the classroom, such as national or federal government officials, or by professionals who are in day-to-day contact with the classroom, such as committees of mainstream and ESL teachers. Others responsible for creating or influencing policy are provincial, state and county government officials, officials of school districts and local educational authorities, school staff, members of teachers' organizations, parent groups and ethnic organizations, and individuals acting as advocates for children. I cannot stress too strongly the need for both mainstream classroom teachers and ESL teachers to become involved in the policy-making machine at one of these levels.

When a particular issue needs to be examined in depth, all four countries have a tradition of establishing a body of inquiry, which is charged with the responsibility of hearing submissions on the issue from both experts in the field and the general public. These bodies then sift through the submissions and formulate recommendations, which are presented to the jurisdiction—usually a municipal, state or provincial, or federal government—that sponsored the inquiry. The government then decides which recommendations to incorporate into official policy.

Unfortunately, the scope of these inquiries is usually quite broad—and ESL education is too often tacked on as an afterthought. Teachers' organizations and individual teachers can play an important role in correcting this situation by presenting well-documented, well-thought-out and well-written briefs. To ensure that they are prepared to influence policy decisions, some school districts have set up continuing work groups with clearly defined tasks in the policy area.

Research into the views of parents of both ESL and non-ESL children, of classroom teachers and ESL teachers, and of counsellors, consultants and administrators may indicate where the educational system is—and is not—meeting the needs of non-English-speaking children and their parents. A review of research and evaluation studies can help remove some of the misconceptions regarding the teaching and learning of English as a second language or dialect. As I listened to a public fo-

34

rum on ESL education on the radio one day, I was concerned to hear parents and teachers condemning the ESL program in their school district because all the students were not able to speak English fluently within a year. They argued that the program should be scrapped because it was clearly inefficient; rather, they said, non-English-speaking students should be placed in regular classrooms to pick up English by osmosis with no additional support for either teachers or students. There was ignorance here that, for the sake of both teachers and children, needed to be replaced by knowledge.

Principles and Policy

Policy statements are often based on a list of principles, which are derived from research or experience or both. From time to time, principles are abandoned and new ones are adopted. Experienced, trained ESL teachers would, I hope, question a principle that said, "The teacher's first aim should be to thoroughly familiarize his pupils with the sounds of the foreign language." This was Article 2 of the International Phonetic Association's declaration of principles of second-language teaching, formulated in the 1880s. It resulted in the teaching of endless sound drills in an isolated context that killed interest. Another questionable principle, this one set out by the well-known behaviourist B.F. Skinner, said, "A language is a set of habits." Skinner used this principle to support the audio-lingual habit theory of second-language learning. Its slogan was Listen and Repeat.

In many of the documents I examined, principles were expressed in the form of a mission statement or a series of beliefs, goals or aims. I reviewed these and grouped them by topic. In doing so, my purpose was to determine which areas are of real importance in the field of ESL and should, therefore, be considered when formulating policy. After all, it is the policy, not the underlying principle or belief, that ultimately affects what happens in schools. My sortie through the approximately 800 documents suggested that the various jurisdictions have developed policies in six major areas:

— The child.
— Access to ESL programs.
— Whole-school language policies.

— Programs and curriculum.
— Diversity, culture and social justice.
— Parents, community and communication.

THE CHILD

In all four countries, there is general agreement that quality education empowers children—and that fluency in oral and written English is necessary if children are to take advantage of opportunities to receive a quality education. There is no agreement, however, on the most effective way of translating these underlying principles into practice. The issue of mainstreaming is an example of how widely opinions can vary. In some jurisdictions, ESL children are mainstreamed from the day they enter an English-speaking school, though most provide at least some help from a trained ESL teacher. It's worth noting, however, that even the definition of a "trained" ESL teacher varies widely. In other jurisdictions, ESL children are placed in a reception or sheltered English class for up to a year before they are mainstreamed.

Bilingual education is another issue on which there is disagreement. Although research shows that educating children in their first and second languages has cognitive and social advantages, many jurisdictions provide no help in the child's first language.

Many of the statements of principle concluded with comments to the effect that ESL children have much to give to their schools and, later, to society. The statements acknowledged that these children have often had experiences beyond the understanding of many of their peers—they have suffered much and seen much, and can help everyone learn the meaning of tolerance and cultural diversity.

ACCESS TO ESL PROGRAMS

I am in complete agreement with the many, many educational authorities whose documents state that students who speak English as a second language are entitled to equal access to all educational opportunities offered by schools, and that ESL students need access to English-language programs in order to succeed in school and society.

36

In my travels, I seldom visited schools that had formulated a language policy for the whole school, perhaps because few jurisdictions explicitly stressed the importance of this. Too often, the ESL program seemed to be an add-on rather than an integral part of the school environment.

Still, documents produced by some jurisdictions did touch on the issue. In a document titled *Language Policy*, Tower Hamlets Local Education Authority in England noted that in order to encourage all children's language development, "teachers need to provide a language-rich environment and the widest possible range of opportunities and contexts for listening, speaking, reading and writing. These will include practical and collaborative activities, when children can use language to communicate with adults and their peers in speech and writing." In addition, a principal wrote to say, "Schools should ensure that all involved in education share a commitment to ensuring that students are enabled to develop an effective command of English."

PROGRAMS AND CURRICULUM

Though few of the documents mandated specific programs, most recommended that ESL students be exposed to the content of the regular curriculum rather than courses dealing almost entirely with aspects of grammar. I was particularly impressed by a statement in *Education for All* (the Swann Report) that said: "Education should involve more than learning about the cultures and lifestyles of various ethnic groups; it should seek to develop in ethnic majority and minority students flexibility of mind, and the ability to analyze critically and rationally the nature of our society within the global context."

DIVERSITY, CULTURE AND SOCIAL JUSTICE

"A language policy must recognize the linguistic and cultural diversity of society," stated the British Columbia Ministry of Education. This belief was also reflected in the materials produced in many other jurisdictions. Some handbooks spoke of the need to develop respect for culture, customs and beliefs, and an understanding of the role of the individual within the family and the family within society. Others suggested that schools should develop the capacity in children to exercise judgment in matters of morality, ethics and social justice, and to build constructive attitudes about human differences and similarities.

PARENTS, COMMUNITY AND COMMUNICATION

The education of immigrant children is influenced by their early settlement experiences and the interaction between the culture of their parents and that of the school and the community. Because language is used to communicate understandings, ideas and feelings and to assist in personal and social development, it was generally agreed that schools should work in close co-operation with both the home and the community.

Policies

I selected the following statements from the documents of the various countries because they seem to represent a strong foundation on which to build a sound and humanitarian ESL policy:

— *Purpose (Canada)*: A language education policy gives direction for future program delivery.
— *Mission statement (Australia)*: Our aim is to enable all students to achieve high standards of learning and to develop self-confidence, optimism, high esteem, respect for others, and achievement of personal excellence.
— *Whole child (Australia)*: We encourage schools and teachers to focus on the development of the whole child as an individual learner and to take into account...motivational, socio-cultural, gender and linguistic factors and the individual learning ability and learning style of each student.
— *Access (U.S.A.)*: It is the policy of this state to provide equal educational opportunities by ensuring that necessary programs are available for ESL pupils while allowing each district maximum flexibility in establishing programs suited to its particular needs.
— *Whole-school language policy (England)*: The Local Education Authority considers that there is a need for all

schools to develop a whole-school language policy. This should be given a high priority.

— *Programs (Canada)*: To facilitate the integration of the student into the regular school program at the earliest possible opportunity, the Department of Education will assist school boards in providing English as a second language programs to students who were born in Canada but who are not fluent in English, and to those who have recently arrived in Canada whose first language is not English.

— *Curriculum (U.S.A.)*: Students must be taught the entire curriculum for their age and grade level, in addition to English.

— *Courses (U.S.A.)*: Fundamental courses may be taught in the pupil's non-English language to support the understanding of concepts, while the ultimate objective shall be to provide a proficiency in those courses in the English language in order that the pupils will be able to participate fully in a society whose language is English.

— *Diversity (Australia)*: Schools and school systems must acknowledge the diversity of backgrounds and circumstances of students from non-English-speaking backgrounds, and take this into account when planning and funding programs.

— *Social justice (England)*: Our policy is to further the Government's fundamental objective that Britain should be a fair and just society where everyone, irrespective of ethnic origin, is able to participate freely and fully in the economic, social and public life of the nation while having the freedom to maintain their own religious identity.

— *Parents (Canada)*: Because schooling is but one aspect of a child's education, schools must work in close cooperation with the home and the community.

— *Community (England)*: It is the policy of the Local Education Authority to ensure that all those involved in education in the Borough—teachers, parents, governors, officers, and members—have a shared understanding of and commitment to celebrating, respecting and fostering the linguistic richness and diversity of the Borough.

The Language of Policies

The strength of a policy—and the level of commitment to carrying it out—can often be measured by its words. Strongly worded policies can have nearly the same impact as laws; indeed, policies are sometimes incorporated into the legislation governing education in various jurisdictions. It is important to note whether strong or weak modals are used to set out a policy and the instructions for implementing it. Strong policies use words like "must," "shall," and "is to," while weak policies use words like "may," "should," "might," "could" and "encourage." A strong modal such as "must" requires a particular action, while a weak modal such as "may" provides more leeway in deciding whether to carry out an action.

Factors Affecting the Implementation of Policies

Even the most practical and strongly worded policies may be difficult to implement successfully for a variety of reasons. For example, a policy may call for trained ESL teachers, but there may not be enough training courses to meet the demand. Within schools, misunderstandings about second-language learning may create negative attitudes about various issues. These may include misconceptions about how quickly a new language can be learned or the necessity of supporting second-language learners so they don't view themselves as failures. Sometimes ESL programs are at the end of the queue when space is allocated—try, for example, teaching oral English in the school library under a sign that reads No Talking! Furthermore, inadequate initial assessment of the students or a failure to monitor their progress can interfere with their ability to master English. In addition, the size of the class, the sensitivity of the teacher and English-speaking students, and, of course, funding all affect the quality of the program.

In addition to sending documents, some respondents outlined the difficulties they face. For example, policies in other areas—special education, psychological assessment, streaming and tracking of students, and so on—can fail to take into account ESL students and, even worse, may discriminate against these students. In some cases, no official policy exists for dealing with ESL students with special needs. Although some jurisdictions handle individual cases by finding *ad hoc* solutions, many would prefer a clearly defined policy. They recognize, however, that developing the resources to carry out such a policy might present a problem.

Some respondents also suggested that ESL and literacy education be recognized as distinct specialist fields.

The single factor with the greatest impact on the successful implementation of policies, however, is funding.

FUNDING

In the years that I worked in ESL, I watched funding formulas come and go and grants to schools rise and fall. No matter what their purpose, educational programs must have stable and adequate funding to be successful. Unfortunately, ESL programs in particular seem to be vulnerable to economic cycles and policy changes that affect funding. ESL programs are often the last to be funded when times are good and the first to be cut when money is tight.

Funding is often affected by the level of public acceptance of ESL programs. From time to time, the cry goes up: "ESL is too costly. Let them learn English before they come here." This, of course, is easier said than done. Much depends on a family's economic situation in their home country and whether English classes are offered in the schools.

Any discussion of ESL funding is also complicated by the fact that some costs are difficult to isolate accurately. In a 1995 report on the Vancouver School Board's ESL services, Alastair Cumming noted the challenge involved in attempting to identify exactly which costs ought to be allocated directly to ESL services. His report said, "Funding and costs for educational services such as ESL are difficult to isolate with precision, because they involve a range of services for those working in areas designated explicitly as ESL together with various indirect costs associated with support services, schooling, administration, and educational services in general."

Funded Programs

Because Australia, England and the United States have national education departments, funding policies for ESL programs in these countries are often set out in national legislation.

Title VII in the United States, for example, provides school districts with money to implement programs for non-English-speaking students. "This money," wrote the Iowa Department of Education, "usually goes to pay the salaries of bilingual program administrators, teachers and teacher aides, to purchase or develop appropriate materials, to offer training for staff and to pay for special services and activities for parents." The Iowa Department of Education has approved funding for the additional costs involved in instructing ESL students, enabling school districts to apply for extra funds when support from federal, state or local sources is either unavailable or inadequate.

The funding of ESL students in England is governed by Section 11 of the Local Government Act, 1966. The stated aim of this act is "to achieve a truly multiracial society." It says that "all citizens, irrespective of ethnic origin, must be able to participate fully and freely in the life of the nation while retaining their own cultural identity." At first, Section 11 provided grants only for students whose country of origin was a member of the British Commonwealth—"with language or customs which differ from those of the rest of the community." In 1993, however, Section 11 was extended to cover all immigrant children, regardless of their country of origin.

Unfortunately, local education authorities are required to bid for the money. Their bids must set out which schools are involved in the project and how staff and resources are to be allocated within schools. In addition, they must include an annual report detailing the previous year's objectives and the results achieved. Preparing a bid involves a great deal of work—with no guarantee that the grant requested will be forthcoming. In fact, the grant is usually less than the amount bid.

According to the Queensland Department of Education in Australia, the federal government provides significant funding through the National Equity Program for Schools. According to the Australian Council of TESOL Associations, a once-only grant of $2,722 (Aus.) was provided for each ESL student in 1994.

In Canada, provincial governments are responsible for all school funding and funding formulas vary across the country. Though some jurisdictions offer no extra funds for ESL programs, most provide a degree of funding in addition to the basic grants allocated for every student in a system. In Saskatchewan, for example, grants for ESL students are provided on a per-capita basis. In 1999, the size of the grant ranged from \$229 to \$531, depending on how much of students' instructional time is devoted to ESL. The Saskatchewan government also provides implementation grants for new programs.

The following list indicates the variety of ESL programs funded in the four countries:

— New arrivals and general support programs.
— ESL and English-as-a-second-dialect classes.
— Refugee programs.
— Heritage or first-language classes.
— ESL specialist teams or language development teams.
— Bilingual education programs.
— Additional educational needs, such as special education or vocational programs.
— Literacy classes.
— Professional development for teachers.
— Teacher training grants for higher education (i.e., for Master's or Doctoral degrees).
— Collecting and disseminating information about successful programs.

In addition, funds may be specifically earmarked for the following:

— Students who match the funding source's definition of an ESL student.
— Students at risk of failure or dropping out.
— Gifted or talented ESL students.
— ESL or bilingual education teachers, aides, consultants, co-ordinators and facilitators.
— Bilingual home-school liaison workers.

Other funding may be available to provide for:

— Start-up costs.
— Release time for ESL and classroom teachers.
— Measures to encourage parental involvement.
— Purchase of ESL materials.
— Purchase of cross-cultural materials.
— Purchase of texts in the first language and English.
— Curriculum development.

When discussing funding, it is as important to examine what is *not* funded as it is to look at what *is* funded. Some jurisdictions do not fund programs for:

— ESL children under nine years old.
— Children who have already received a specified number of hours of instruction (e.g., 100) or a specified number of years of instruction (e.g., one).
— Children born in the country in which they are receiving instruction, but whose first language is not English.
— Pre-school and kindergarten children.
— Children attending schools whose ESL population does not meet a required minimum for establishing a program (e.g., a jurisdiction may require a population of 15 ESL students before a program is funded).

Funding Formulas

To try to ensure that funds are directed appropriately, some jurisdictions have instituted points systems. These take into consideration a variety of factors:

— *Geographic origin*: Students from non-English-speaking countries in Europe, Asia, Africa, South America and Central America may be assigned more points than students from English-speaking countries in North America, the British Isles, Australia and New Zealand.
— *Date of arrival*: Recently arrived ESL students may be assigned more points that those who entered the school system one or two years earlier.

In addition, funding formulas may be based on the following:

— *Language instruction weighting factor*: This requires school districts to consider the full-time equivalent of co-ordinators, consultants, self-contained and resource teachers employed in ESL programs, the cost of language instruction programs, and the additional cost to the district of providing language programs.
— *Unit breakdowns that take into account the number of ESL students*: Under a formula like this, for example, a minimum unit of six pupils may be entitled to one teacher, as well as six per cent of the salary of the average teacher in the jurisdiction. A maximum unit of 20 pupils may be

entitled to one teacher, as well as eight per cent of the salary of the average teacher in the jurisdiction and the salary of half a teacher's aide. Units of 7 to 12 pupils and 13 to19 pupils receive funding at a level between the minimum and maximum.

— *Hourly calculations*: Some jurisdictions pay teachers to provide a specific number of hours of instruction at a specified hourly rate.

— *Competitive bidding*: Schools or school districts in England engage in a bidding process that requires them to submit detailed requests for funding that include a description of the program's purpose and design, the number of students involved, and so on.

No matter what specific funding formula is in effect in a particular jurisdiction, it will be affected by the grant ceiling—the maximum amount of money the funding agency will provide.

Funding Criteria

To be eligible for funds, schools or school districts must usually meet certain criteria. For example, they may be required to:

— Conduct a home language survey.
— Conduct an initial assessment of students identified as ESL.
— Monitor students' progress.
— Evaluate ESL programs.
— Assign responsibilities to specific individuals.
— Hire qualified ESL teachers for the program.
— Write separate and precise contracts for ESL teachers and aides.
— Report on students' achievements to parents and ESL co-ordinators or facilitators.
— Establish entrance and exit criteria for the ESL program.
— Design a program of instruction to meet the educational needs of students identified as ESL and outline how ESL teachers and bilingual assistants will be deployed to meet those needs.
— Be accountable for the success or failure of the program.

During the last half of the 20th century, the cost of educating all children rose steadily—and sometimes dramatically—in all four countries. Three major factors contributed to this: an increase in the number of children attending school; an increase in teachers' salaries; and an increase in operating costs, which include everything from buying textbooks to paying the bills for heating and lighting school buildings.

When people lobby for tax reductions, education is often singled out for cuts so that governments can reduce expenditures—and the two areas of education often considered the most expendable are special education and ESL. This is regrettable, because the very children who need special education or ESL instruction are often those who are the least likely to experience success without the help of well-trained teachers.

The group best qualified to speak out on behalf of these children is the local or national teachers' organization. A teacher's work extends far beyond the classroom, and I hope that the matters touched on in this book will help you carry out the very important task of ensuring that every child receives the best possible education.

. . . . 3

STUDENTS

Language minority students attending public schools must be given a meaningful opportunity to participate in and benefit from educational programming at school.

Superintendent of Schools
Vermont

I recently had dinner with six teachers who had taken an introductory course in teaching English as a second language that I taught in the 1970s and early '80s. Since that time, one had retired, two had returned to the classroom after a stint as ESL consultants (their jobs were terminated when funding for ESL was cut), one was back in the classroom after taking time out to raise a family, and two had taught ESL continuously since their student-teacher days. All spoke of their delight in teaching ESL and felt it was the best job in the school system. "Why?" I wanted to know. Their responses boiled down to the fact that they were keen on teaching and the students were keen on learning.

The course I taught—An Introduction to Teaching English as a Second Language—was not mandatory; no one had been required to take it. As a result, those who enrolled did so because they wanted to learn. During my 21 years as an instructor of prospective ESL teachers, about a third of those I taught had themselves been non-English-speaking immigrant children. For some, learning English and adjusting to a new culture had been a good experience; for others, the experience had not been so good. All were motivated to become ESL teachers themselves by a desire to make the experience of arriving in a new country a positive one for others—and they believed that their own experiences, combined with the knowledge they gained from my course, could help them do just that.

They agreed that ESL students *want* to learn English and *want* to be a part of both the school community and the local community. They spoke appreciatively of the telephone calls and letters they continue to receive from former students who want to pass along news of their successes—and, sometimes, their failures. The bond between teacher and student has remained strong.

This chapter focuses on ESL students themselves. It discusses how a second language is both acquired and learned, as well as students' backgrounds. It also examines how the four countries identify, assess, place and track the progress of students who need ESL instruction.

Acquiring and Learning a Second Language

Language is *acquired* when students are immersed in the target language, a phenomenon that occurs naturally when children master their first language. Language is *learned* when students are explicitly taught grammar and structures. Because it is necessary to both acquire and learn a second language in order to become fluent in it, both processes are necessary. As a result, ESL students must be encouraged to participate in classroom activities, problem solving, experiments and so on in a context that is both interesting and authentic. Teachers can use these activities to focus on aspects of the language that students need to learn.

A program handbook published by the Scarborough Board of Education, which is now part of the Toronto District School Board in Ontario, described the enormity of the task facing ESL students: "They must acquire vocabulary that has both range and depth, including idioms, homonyms and figurative language; they must become familiar with the sound system of English, including phonology, stress, intonation, and pitch, and they must internalize the structure of English, which is a complex mixture of word order, sentence patterns, and sentence transformations. Not only must the students understand what is being said, but they must also be able to respond. They have to hear language (receptive function), process and interpret (integrative function), and respond (expressive function). What they say must be appropriate to the social situation, have the meaning the speaker intends, and communicate this meaning clearly."

In Massachusetts, the Department of Education pointed out that the teaching of English must extend beyond the walls of the English classroom: "Language and cognitive development are closely related and fundamental; they should be continually stimulated in both (or all) of the languages spoken by linguistic minority pupils. Language development should be a conscious part of teaching in math and science as much as in 'language arts,' and all teachers should possess appropriate insight and skills in this area."

There is general agreement that language is acquired most effectively when it is used in academic and social contexts that give ESL students the opportunity to figure out how English works; that is, they need to be in a language-rich environment in which they are using language to fulfil real purposes.

Many of the documents produced in the four countries acknowledge this. For example, guidelines published in the Canadian province of Alberta say: "It is necessary for teachers to understand the linguistic, social, cultural and psychological implications for students learning English as a second language. Knowledge of second-language acquisition and the effects it can have on the personal and academic development of ESL students is also essential. This knowledge will help teachers to plan a suitable program and develop effective methods of instruction for ESL students in the regular classroom and in an ESL class."

Individual jurisdictions within the four countries outline a variety of approaches to and views of learning English as a second language. Though the terminology may differ, all the approaches acknowledge the importance of using language in authentic contexts.

— *Meaning-based language learning*: Language activities focus on making meaning, rather than on coming up with the "right" answer, which is often a rote response to an isolated question. This approach encourages students to use language to explore ideas, pose questions and debate issues.
— *Context-based language learning*: This approach suggests that meaning-making activities occur when a commu-

nity of learners communicate and collaborate in authentic learning contexts that enable teachers and students to be sensitive to differences in language and culture.

— *Language-based learning*: To help them learn their second language, students are encouraged to draw on all their available linguistic and non-linguistic resources, including the cultural, language and literacy experiences they have had in their first language.

— *Humanity-based language learning*: If students from diverse backgrounds view both the learning environment and themselves positively, it will help them feel secure and free to experiment and take risks with their newfound knowledge.

— *Language for learning*: Because language is essential for thinking and learning, learning activities in all program areas should be designed to help students develop the language skills they need to think, learn and communicate effectively.

Effective ESL teachers plan lessons that are meaningful to the students. They use a variety of key visuals and activities, try to make all statements comprehensible to students, act as an appropriate language model for students, and look for opportunities to encourage students to interact with their classmates. In an article published in *TESOL Quarterly*, Christian Faltis and Sarah Hudelson wrote: "We believe that language and literacy learning in schools results from understanding and participating in social interaction with classmates and the teacher about topics that matter to both the teacher and the students."

One problem facing some ESL students is the steadily increasing number of non-English speaking students enrolling in schools. In some jurisdictions, this has led to an absence of native-English-speaking students who can provide the opportunities ESL students need to interact in English.

ESL students learn in a variety of ways and at different rates, as do their English-speaking peers. Some are proficient language learners and some are not. For all students, learning is both an individual and a group process. Some ESL students may remain silent for what may seem like an unnaturally long time. During this period, many are still absorbing the language. When they feel ready to talk, their knowledge of vocabulary and sentence structure may surprise listeners.

Is it possible to recognize a proficient language learner? The Catholic Education Office of Sydney, Australia, noted that a proficient language learner "is happy, relaxed, confident, outgoing, willing to take risks, willing to make mistakes. Not all students have such dispositional traits and it is therefore important to do what you can to encourage them, particularly with children who are new to the school." Those who do not display traits such as these may need counselling in their first language to give them encouragement and hope by helping them understand that they are going through a process and that it takes time to master a second language. ESL students should always be viewed in terms of *what they can do* and *what they know*, not in terms of what they cannot do and what they do not know. They are not deficient in language; indeed, they may speak more languages than their monolingual English-speaking peers. They just don't speak English well—yet!

Proficiency in acquiring a second language may also be influenced by attitudes. For example, the difference between the way ESL students—and their parents—expect schools to operate and actual classroom practice in English-speaking countries can be a source of conflict. The scene is set for misunderstanding if parents and children expect a male authoritarian teacher who believes in rote learning, but are faced with a female teacher who believes in collaborative problem-solving and enquiry. On quite a different note, however, many societies automatically accord teachers considerably more respect than is customary in some English-speaking countries, a situation that often helps teachers and students form a strong, productive learning relationship.

Age also affects the speed at which a second language is acquired. In an article that appeared in *TESOL Quarterly*, Virginia P. Collier made the following generalizations about the relationship between students' prospects for success in acquiring a second language and their age at the time they are first exposed to a second language:

— In children who have not yet reached puberty, the age at which they are first exposed to—or receive instruction in—the second language does not affect their prospects of achieving academic success, as long as their cognitive development in their first language is continued until they are 12 (the age by which acquisition of the first language is largely complete).

— When children's development in their first language is discontinued before it is complete, it may have a negative effect on their cognitive development in a second language. Conversely, children who have achieved full cognitive development in two languages enjoy cognitive advantages over children who are monolingual.

— In the early stages of acquiring a second language, adults and adolescents whose cognitive development in their first language is solid master basic interpersonal communicative skills faster than children. After two or three years of exposure to the second language, however, children begin to outpace adults and adolescents in this area. Many adults and adolescents, for example, retain an accent.

— Children aged 8 to 12 who have been schooled in their first language for several years tend to acquire a second language most efficiently. Although adolescents with solid schooling in their first language acquire a second language equally efficiently, pronunciation often remains a problem for them.

This age-related difference in the ability to acquire a second language can significantly affect academic achievement, as the following policies and guidelines issued by the education department of Queensland, Australia, acknowledge:

— Older students face stiffer academic demands as they are trying to master a second language.

— With younger children, English may take over as the language in which linguistic and cognitive development takes place. Sometimes, development in their first language comes to a stop while they struggle to make sense of their new language. As a result, they may be trapped in a semi-lingual state in which neither language is developed fluently.

The Importance of Identifying ESL Students

In general, ESL students are defined as those who speak a language other than English at home for the greater part of the day, and whose limited proficiency in English is likely to affect their prospects of achieving academic success. Although many ESL students are, in fact, born overseas, it isn't unusual for them to have been born in the country where they are being schooled. Some may have even come from another English-speaking country or another area of the same country. Some years ago, for example, I sat in on an ESL class in a small town on the Canadian prairies. To my consternation and, I must confess, amusement, a nine-year-old who had just arrived from Scotland sat among children from Europe and Asia. His Scottish brogue was so thick that no one could understand him!

At first glance, students who sit quietly in class and respond appropriately to simple questions like "What is your name?" may seem to be getting along just fine. But failing to recognize that these students need support in both learning a new language and adjusting to a new culture may prevent them from either receiving the education they are entitled to or participating fully in extracurricular activities and community events. Furthermore, accurately identifying ESL students often means that they can be helped by other students with the same background. What a relief it must be for a newly enrolled ESL student to receive a helping hand from another who shares the same linguistic and cultural background!

The accurate identification of ESL students is also important because it often affects the funding of programs. Successful programs cannot be established unless information about ESL students is collected, tabulated and updated regularly.

About 30 years ago, I attended a meeting of school trustees who were—at last!—concerned because it appeared that their schools were full of ESL students, though only a small number were receiving language support. I rose and suggested that before planning a new ESL program, they ought to find out how many ESL students in the schools needed help, which schools these students attended, and their ages. I sat down and the trustees moved on to another topic. My comment, I thought, had been ignored.

Later that evening, however, one of the trustees phoned and asked how they could count ESL students. I told him. A count was conducted, and trustees, administrators and the Ministry of Education were shocked to find out just how many ESL students were enrolled in their schools—and how few were receiving the support they needed. Funds were found and a program was initiated. That school board now has a good program; as good, that is, as current funding cuts allow.

In most jurisdictions today, a screening process is in place to identify students for whom English is a second language. The process usually has four objectives:

— To identify students whose first language is not English or whose dialect is a Creole or non-standard English dialect, and to determine their level of proficiency in standard English.
— To determine the kind of English-language support program students need.
— To determine the kind and level of content instruction students require.
— To determine the level of first-language support required for students destined for placement in bilingual programs whose aim is to produce students fluent in both their first language and English.

One of the most important tools used in this screening process is a survey of the language—or languages—spoken by the child in the home to parents, siblings, grandparents and friends. Administered to all newly enrolling students, a home language survey asks questions designed to elicit information about a student's background. The information sought may cover the following:

— The age at which the child learned to talk.
— The language the child first acquired.
— Other languages the child knows.
— The primary language used in the child's home.
— The language spoken to parents, siblings, friends and grandparents.
— The language used most often.

The East Sussex County Council in Southern England, for example, suggests that schools need information about the following:

- The cultural and ethnic origins of the child and family.
- The language(s) spoken at home.
- The child's previous school experience.
- The child's level of literacy in the first language.
- The access the child has had to English.
- The child's religious, cultural, dietary and special health needs.
- The name and telephone number of a person willing to interpret for the child, if necessary.
- Other relevant information about the child's interests, abilities, etc.
- Relevant documents, such as report cards, visa, etc.

Some jurisdictions also identify "booster" students. These are usually recent immigrants who, because of war, civil unrest, poverty or an inadequate school system in their homeland, are academically behind their English-speaking peers and need special help to catch up. Some of these students may even be illiterate in their first language. The goal is to enable them to fit comfortably into a mainstream class with children their own age.

In addition to a home language survey, the identification process usually involves an interview, conducted in their first language, with the child and his or her parents or guardians. In addition, documents relating to the child's immigration status and previous schooling are reviewed and the child's proficiency in English is assessed.

Students arrive in their new country at various ages from a variety of backgrounds and with a variety of experiences. Some may have immigrated with parents who are seeking a better economic and educational future for themselves and their children, while others may be religious or political refugees. Although those who fall into the first category can probably return home if and when they please, refugees usually can't. Young children may not understand why they have been torn away from relatives and friends to live in a country where the language and customs are so different. In fleeing their country, some children have had horrendous experiences. They may have seen people they love subjected to piracy, rape, murder or imprisonment, and may have lived for months or years in refugee camps with inadequate educational facilities.

As a result, some ESL children take longer than others to learn English, develop study skills, and acquire the body of knowledge necessary to prepare them to enter a mainstream classroom. Counselling in a student's first language may be needed to resolve emotional problems. Students' sight and hearing should also be checked, so that appropriate action can be taken if necessary.

For some ESL children, life in their new country is tough. In a pamphlet designed to help schools understand and welcome refugees, the Redbridge Education Authority in England described some of the horrors these children had experienced: "The refugee child may well have been through the same traumas as the adults in her/his family. One small boy became hysterical when he saw a dead rabbit on the road and said it reminded him of the dead people he had seen on the streets of Beirut."

In an article in *The Globe and Mail*, a Canadian teacher talked about children from war-torn parts of the world who carry their nightmares with them and act them out in class: "They are so traumatized. All of a sudden they're off this plane into a classroom with nothing. No language, nothing to help them integrate into the country. A little girl who spends her first week in school cowering under the desk, trembling with fear. A boy who spends all day mimicking the action of an anti-aircraft battery, the most prominent feature of his former neighbourhood. Another boy who continually defecates in the hallway."

Education News, a newsletter published in Victoria, Australia, printed the thoughts of 10-year-old Phal, who had attended school in Cambodia for just one year before arriving in her new country. Phal couldn't read or write in her own language, but after a year in an English-language school, she was able to express how it felt to be a new arrival: "Why I am scared to go to school. Because I don't know about school. And I don't know English very good. I don't have friends too. And writing very slow, I am outside a class I very, very scared because don't know about English and mathematic, geography not very good. And bell is gone I am go inside but I don't know which class. I go office to asked teacher, I go home. I am scared to go to school."

While ESL students are undoubtedly different from their English-speaking counterparts, they also share many characteristics with them. They have mastered a language and learned what language can do for them. They have a knowledge of how to behave in their own culture. They have varying abilities, interests and backgrounds: some are gifted and some have special needs. They may have attended school in their home country and some of these school experiences may be similar to those of their new country. In some subject areas, they may have more knowledge than their new peers; in others, they may have less.

Some ESL students come from school systems that have prepared them well academically; their greatest need is to learn English quickly so they can join the mainstream. At the other end of the spectrum are students from poor countries where educational opportunities have been limited. These students often require a great deal of help for a long time. They are the ones most likely to experience school as a hostile and unwelcoming place unless every effort is made to shore up their self-esteem. In between are most ESL students who know some English and some subject matter. Given appropriate help, they will, over time, do well.

One group that merits special mention is adolescents, for they face special challenges. Not only are they coping with the physical, social, intellectual and emotional changes that are part of growing up, but they are learning a new language and adapting to a new culture at the same time. This subjects them to added stress at a time of life that is already very stressful.

"Many LEP teenagers have to work to support themselves, to contribute to their families, and often to provide money to send to family members back in their home country," wrote BW Associates, a consulting group hired to evaluate ESL programs for adolescents in California. In addition, their parents may be struggling to adapt to the new culture, to learn English, and to find employment, and some are not able to give their children the support they need. In some families, it becomes financially necessary for the mother, for the first time, to work outside the home. One teenager told me: "Before we emigrated, my parents were interested in what I did. Now their only interest is to make money and to buy everything they think Canadians have. I wish we could go home."

Teenage immigrants, who have probably learned English faster than their parents, may find themselves taking on responsibilities that are normally assumed by adults—acting as a translator, filling out forms, and dealing with various public agencies. All this takes time, and time is short for ESL students who arrive in their adopted country in their teen years. If they do not have enough time to master both English and curriculum content by the time they graduate from high school, their ability to take advantage of further educational opportunities may be curtailed, unless special courses are available to meet their needs. This can have a dramatic impact on their attitude. Teenagers who hold out little hope for their future and who are not able to communicate well with their parents or another significant adult may start skipping school, getting into fights, engaging in criminal behaviour, or joining gangs. Some parents may be reluctant to deal with aberrant behaviour because it is regarded as the school's responsibility in their home culture. Some teenage students live a lonely life on their own with only distant adult supervision.

Furthermore, as parents search for employment, the family may end up moving frequently, which may interfere with children's academic and social progress and contribute to a sense of instability within the family. During this time, teenagers and their parents must try to bridge the gap between their home culture and the new culture. How much of the new culture must they adopt in order to be accepted by their peers? How much of their home culture must they retain in order to continue to be the person they were before they emigrated? Though I have lived in Canada for 50 years, I still pronounce words like "path" and "fast" as "pahth" and "fahst" and I drive on "dual carriageways"—I wouldn't be me if I didn't!

Reception and Orientation

"You never get a second chance to make a first impression" runs an advertising slogan for a shampoo. The same is true of schools, where the first few minutes can be crucial. If the school seems to be a welcoming place, ESL parents and children may be reassured that the experiences that await them are likely to be positive. Many jurisdictions, believing that the initial reception, assessment and orientation of ESL children is so important that it should not be left to school secretaries or very busy ESL teachers, have established reception and orientation centres where ESL students can be assessed and introduced to their new schools.

The Oakridge Reception and Orientation Centre in Vancouver, British Columbia, for example, processes more than 4,000 new arrivals a year, about 800 of them in the summer months of July and August. The centre, for which I am delighted to take some credit, was established in 1988 after Jim Cummins, Jean Handscombe and I wrote a report identifying the need for such a facility.

The centre's multilingual staff is capable of assessing most newcomers in both their first language and English so that the children can be placed in the appropriate school and program. In addition, the centre can call on a variety of agencies to help newcomers with settlement problems and find interpreters when no staff member speaks a particular language. A community health nurse is available to check on health matters and give advice.

Many reception centres prepare a welcome packet in the first language of the family. In the state of Georgia, for example, the packet provides information about the school, the community, the cost of meals at the school, the availability of special meal programs, attendance rules, immunization requirements, the school calendar, the availability of transportation to and from school, and the parent-teacher organization. Families also receive a card containing the name of the interviewer, the address and phone number of the school or reception centre, and the name and room number of the child's ESL teacher. Finally, if appropriate, the family is taken on a tour of the school or the centre.

Other items that might be covered are the school's attendance expectations and how to report absences, the report card system, holidays, school rules and expectations for students' conduct, fire drills, assemblies, passes to leave class, extracurricular activities, and how parents can take advantage of opportunities to talk to the teacher.

Besides providing an introduction to the school, the orientation process in Moncton, New Brunswick, helps parents become familiar with the geography of the community and shows them how to carry out day-to-day tasks such as buying groceries, going to the bank, post office or library, using public transit, and gaining access to medical services. Families are also provided with basic information about the host culture, such as the dates of public holidays, what kind of weather to expect, and the significance of current events.

One excellent program established at two middle schools in Seattle, Washington, in the early 1990s was a bilingual intervention team. The two schools were served by a consulting teacher and two student advocates. A 1992 year-end report noted that the members of the team "worked closely with building administrators, counsellors and teachers of both bilingual and mainstream classes. They targeted middle school students who are at greatest risk of school failure or drop-out and served nearly all bilingual students in the buildings. Services provided to students include tutoring, help in completing assignments, help with reading and study skills, counselling, help in understanding the American school system, home contacts and a broad range of other assistance." The report concluded that the program had met its goals of helping at-risk students stay in school and achieve success in their classes. One indication of the program's success was the increased call for the team's services in both schools.

A Child and Family Consultation Centre located in Loxford Hall in Redbridge, England, was described in a 1995 edition of the *Redbridge Schools' Refugee Newsletter*. The newsletter noted that the multi-disciplinary team of professionals who staff the centre are "qualified and experienced in assessing and treating children and young people with emotional, relationship or behavioural difficulties. The staff group are used to working with children and families to discover their strengths and stresses, involving them in working towards resolving or reducing their difficulties. Many refugee families show admirable resilience in coping with sudden enforced changes and losses in their lives. However, some children may prove to be seriously affected by such disruption—sometimes by traumatic memories. First line staff, perhaps especially teachers, can be very helpful in identifying those who may need additional therapeutic help."

Traumatic memories can sometimes be triggered unexpectedly. I recall a Vancouver teenager who refused to go on a class excursion to see the British Columbia government in action because it would have meant taking a ferry to Victoria, where the provincial legislature is located. He and his parents had been among the Vietnamese boat people who had eventually arrived in Canada. He wanted nothing more to do with boats!

Assessors and Assessment

Accurately assessing the English-language proficiency of ESL students entering the school system and monitoring the progress of those who are already part of the system is very important. Hugh South, of the National Association for Language Development in the Curriculum in England, wrote: "Assessment of (English as an additional language) is absolutely central to teaching and learning. It should be a driving force in taking forward the teaching and learning of EAL pupils and therefore their achievement."

Many jurisdictions have acknowledged the importance of the assessment process by establishing policies to govern the way it is carried out. In Texas, for example, school districts are required to offer bilingual education and special language programs and to establish a language proficiency assessment committee. The committee must include a professional bilingual educator, a professional transitional language educator, a parent of an ESL student, and a campus administrator. The committee begins by reviewing all pertinent information about the students. Then it recommends the most appropriate placement, reviews each student's progress at the end of the school year to determine future placements, monitors the progress of students who have left bilingual or special language programs, designates the most appropriate placement for these students, and determines whether an extended program—one beyond the regular school—is appropriate.

In Maine, the Department of Education suggests that the responsibilities of language-assessment committees include notifying parents in a language they comprehend of the date and nature of English-language proficiency testing, meeting with the staff of schools to provide information about ESL students and support services, and monitoring students' progress for three years after they leave ESL programs.

The Peel Region Board of Education in Ontario has introduced a team approach to meeting the needs of ESL students. The team includes the classroom teacher and the ESL teacher, as well as teachers of subjects such as music, physical education and French. The team is involved in both assessing and evaluating the progress of the ESL students. A profile of the student's learning is shared with the student, parents, teachers and administrators.

In Massachusetts, the Department of Education introduced an eight-point procedure for identifying and classifying ESL students. In each school district, an individual or language assessment committee is charged with responsibility for:

— Identifying ESL students and assessing their language-learning needs.
— Ensuring that ESL students are placed in appropriate programs.
— Meeting periodically with relevant bilingual, ESL and standard curriculum staff to determine whether students are ready for partial or full-time mainstreaming.
— Developing and implementing appropriate procedures for reclassifying bilingual students according to their language proficiency.
— Monitoring the follow-up activities for partially and fully mainstreamed students.
— Recommending instructional or other services for partially and fully mainstreamed students.
— Developing a process for informing relevant bilingual, ESL or standard curriculum staff of students' progress.
— Establishing a record-keeping system for tracking assessment results, instructional placement, reclassification procedures, and follow-up monitoring activities.

Despite the excellent initiatives undertaken in many jurisdictions, not all ESL students are appropriately assessed. Some are placed in schools with little, if any, formal assessment because administering and marking tests takes time—something that administrators aren't always willing to provide.

In an address to delegates to the 1995 ACTA-ATESOL conference in Sydney, Australia, Stephanie Burton zeroed in on the shortcomings of some assessment processes: "A common mistake made by administrative personnel is that they may assume that a limited oral exchange in a highly routinized situation is indicative of proficiency. The other staff have to cope with the results of this mistake when they discover that the student has an outstanding ability to nod in all the right places without being able to follow much at all. The poor student may be accused of a pathological tendency to pretend that they understand but are just unwilling to comply with orders!"

A final word. During the assessment process, care must be taken to prevent ESL students from being identified as needing "special education." The Ministry of Education for Western Australia warns that when tests or criteria are heavily English-language-based and reflect the culture of the host country, ESL students may be "incorrectly assessed by teachers, school psychologists and other school personnel."

At the same time, every effort must be made to identify academically gifted students. "It is imperative," says the Pennsylvania Department of Education, "for school districts to reevaluate the fairness of their procedures for the identification of gifted (culturally and linguistically diverse) students, since instruments that are typically used to assess giftedness are constructed in English and emphasize linguistic skills."

How are these students identified? In Philadelphia, Pennsylvania, identification depends on the observations of the teacher and parents, who "may be able to describe cognitive skills and achievements among students who are (culturally and linguistically diverse). When evaluating a student who is CLD suspected of being gifted, it is recommended to observe closely the following three major areas: (a) rapid accumulation and assimilation of knowledge in English and the native language, (b) leadership abilities and (c) interpersonal sensitivity."

Assessment Tools

The various jurisdictions tend to use a mix of assessment tools, both formal and informal.

One formal assessment tool that often sparks controversy is standardized tests. In a document titled *Social Justice in Education*, the Western Australia Ministry of Education expressed a concern shared by many jurisdictions: that standardized tests place ESL students at a disadvantage because they possess neither the knowledge of English nor the familiarity with school subject matter required to perform well. "Performance in such tests, therefore, should not be used as a measure of the student's overall academic ability," the document warned—a warning that should be heeded by all who interpret these tests.

In addition, ESL students may be apprehensive and insecure during their first days in a new school, feelings that are likely to interfere with their performance. As a result, it is a good idea to wait until students feel more at home before administering a standardized test.

When standardized tests are used, the instrument selected varies from country to country and often from jurisdiction to jurisdiction within the countries. The tests mentioned most often were the California Achievement Test, the California Test of Basic Skills, the Iowa Test of Basic Skills, the Language Assessment Scale and the Stanford Achievement Test, all of which originate in the United States. Many jurisdictions told me, however, that they make up their own tests or use only carefully selected parts of the tests mentioned, such as the vocabulary section.

One of the most important informal assessment tools is the observations of teachers. In a document titled *Better English as a Second Language*, the Maryland State Department of Education noted: "Teachers who regularly observe and assess their limited-English proficient students' actual oral language and literacy performance and who use this information to guide their instruction promote learning because this information is one of the most accurate indicators of these students' current abilities and needs."

The Catholic Education Office in Sydney, Australia, takes this idea a step farther. Its guidelines say: "Assessment procedures must be congruent with teaching practice. The ESL resource teacher can play a key role in monitoring and assessment procedures by suggesting to mainstream teachers ways in which to gather samples of students' oral and written language in action, and by drawing teachers' attention to the language development needs of their ESL students which the samples reveal. Assessment is effective when teachers use the new information gained as a basis for program design."

In addition to the observations of teachers, the most frequently mentioned informal assessment tools are paper-and-pencil tests created by staff, story retelling, dictation, and informal interviews. Even these assessment tools must be used carefully, however. The Iowa Department of Education, for example, instructs teachers to "make an effort to focus assessments on the content and not on the LEP student's use of the English language. In addition, the teacher must also make an effort to design alternative forms of assessment that will allow the student to demonstrate his or her learning in a manner that downplays the role of English language use."

Assessing the Assessment Process

To ensure that the assessment process is fair and accurate, the East Sussex County Council in England believes that the following questions should be asked every time a child completes a test of English competence:

— Did the child fully understand the task, and what was expected of him or her?
— Would the child have benefited from practical demonstration, or more support through illustration?
— Were there enough non-verbal messages in the setting up of the task so that the pupil could proceed?
— Was the task appropriate to the cultural experience of the child?
— Was it possible to record achievement other than by verbal or written means (e.g., through drawing, graphs, etc.)?
— Could the home language have been used as part of the task (e.g., labelling objects in the first language and English)?
— If there is another speaker of the same language in the class, would the child have benefited from discussing the task in the first language?
— Would the child have benefited from more work in pairs or groups to allow further discussion in English?

Other factors can also influence assessment results and should be considered. According to the Language Support Service of Barking and Dagenham, England, other questions that should be asked are:

— Is the pupil experiencing overt or covert racism?
— What is the pupil's previous schooling?
— Does the child receive any extra help (e.g., from friends, neighbours and peers, as well as family)?
— What is the level of proficiency in the child's first language?
— What is the child's school attendance like?

- Does the child attend any after-school classes?
- How does the child behave at home? Talk to the parents to discuss their concerns.
- Have all sensible medical checks been carried out (e.g., if the child squints and has trouble reading print, does she or he need a vision test)?
- Are any other support services involved?
- Does the child attend a community or religious school after regular school hours?
- Has the progress of the child been discussed with the local support service or a bilingual teacher?

Assessing Children's Proficiency in Their First Language

In addition to assessing students' English-language proficiency, many jurisdictions require that their proficiency in their first language also be evaluated. Arizona, for example, requires an assessment of students' ability to comprehend, speak, read and write their first language using specific tests and procedures approved by the state board of education. The assessments must be conducted by "individuals who are proficient in the particular language and who have been thoroughly trained to administer and score the test or procedure."

Similarly, the Los Angeles Unified School District requires that all Spanish-speaking ESL students be assessed in their first language using the Spanish Language Assessment Scales. The results are used to determine each Spanish-speaking ESL student's program placement.

In Portland, Oregon, schools are encouraged to recommend that students continue to use their first language at home and at school because:

- It supplies background knowledge, which makes English instruction more understandable.
- It enhances the development of basic literacy because it is easier to learn to read in a language one already knows; we learn to read once only.
- High-level literacy skills in the first language support high-level literacy skills in the second language.
- No empirical evidence supports the view that time spent on the first language detracts from the development of the second language. If anything, greater elabo-

ration of the first language results in more efficient acquisition of the second language.
— Comparisons of bilingual and monolingual children, as well as comparisons of bilingual children of varying levels of development, indicate that bilingualism can lead to superior performance in a variety of intellectual skills.
— One of the most fundamental assumptions underlying the efficiency of bilingual instruction is that skills and knowledge learned in the first language transfer to English, the second language.
— Bilingual students frequently switch between two languages during conversations. This is a normal occurrence and does not lead to confusion.

Placement

The appropriate placement of students is critical if they are to thrive in their new school. When deciding where individual students should be placed, many factors must be considered.

In its program guidelines, New York State reminds schools that they "must keep in mind that (limited English proficient) students arrive at school with a wide range of academic skills. Some students may be starting school in kindergarten and others may be continuing an education begun under an entirely different educational system. Some LEP students are gifted, others need remediation or special educational services. Some bring good native language skills, while others have low levels of literacy in their native languages. Most LEP students are average achievers, as are mainstream English proficient students. All are limited in their proficiency in the English language and may be categorized along a continuum of their English language development."

In Liverpool, England, the Bilingual Development Service and Consultancy suggests: "Placements in classes need to be according to a flexible set of criteria related to the school's own system. Vertically grouped classes can provide a lot of variety in terms of stimulus and opportunity. It is possible to provide this flexibility with a range of role models for language use and learning styles in other kinds of classes. There needs to be a balance between plenty of opportunity for play, discovery and talk (both social and on task) and a certain level of formality. Some children expect more formality in school contexts than the free play of early years classrooms would seem to suggest and this can lead to misunderstandings."

ESL students need to be placed with other students their own age, something that is underlined by the Maine Department of Education. "Under no circumstances should a student be placed in a grade level that is more than one year below his/her chronological age. Although it may seem logical to place a language minority child at a grade level that matches the kind of English skills he/she appears to need to acquire, it would be a great disservice to the child both socially and cognitively to do so."

An administrator once asked me whether it would be all right to place a 13-year-old girl in Grade 1 because she spoke no English. After peeling myself off the ceiling, I very firmly said, "No! I can accept one year below grade level but no more."

Particular caution must be exercised when deciding whether to place ESL students in special education programs. This must not be done only on the basis of criteria that measure and evaluate English-language proficiency. Those conducting the assessment must take care to determine whether a child has a learning problem in addition to a lack of facility in English. If this is the conclusion, the special education program selected for the child must address both the learning problem and the child's need to learn English.

Many jurisdictions make special mention of the risks involved in funnelling non-English-speaking children into special education programs and specifically warn against it. The Maine Department of Education, for example, says: "Since limited English proficiency is not a handicapping condition, limited English proficient students should not be placed in any special education program unless an exceptionality is well-documented and evaluated and appropriate procedures (e.g., linguistic background examined) have been followed."

This caution is echoed by the Iowa Department of Education: "It is possible that the LEP student suspected of experiencing difficulty in learning does not actually have a learning disability, but is going through a period of social, psychological and/or linguistic adjustment. Cultural differences in learning styles and strategies, as well as social and cultural in-

68

teraction patterns with peers and teachers, do not constitute a learning disability."

Record Keeping

Once a child has been placed in an ESL program, it is imperative to monitor her or his progress for three years to ensure that the right placement has been made and the right program drawn up and followed. To ensure that this monitoring is effective, it is important to keep records of children's progress.

The Maine Department of Education recommends keeping a language-progress file for each ESL student. It suggests that the file include:

— All test scores pertaining to program decisions.
— Recommendations for the individual child's program.
— Portfolio of literacy work done by the student.
— An individual learning program setting out the program's goals, objectives and outcomes.
— A copy of the home language survey that initially identified the child as requiring ESL placement.
— Parent interview or questionnaire notes.
— Timeline of language assessment committee meetings.
— Recommendations for reclassification or exit from program.
— Notes from observations by school staff.

Effective records also help researchers expand our knowledge and understanding of ESL students. The Oakridge Reception and Orientation Centre in Vancouver, British Columbia, has information on about 25,000 students. In 1997, Lee Gunderson drew on information in these records to produce a document titled *Some Findings about School-Age Immigrants in Vancouver*. Of the 60 points he listed, I found the following particularly interesting:

— On average, students spent two and a half years in ESL classes.
— Score on a nine-item test of prepositions was the best predictor of reading comprehension.
— Knowledge of the names of the letters of the alphabet was a poor predictor of reading comprehension.

— About one in 20 immigrant students appears to have learning difficulties.
— After six years of schooling, students' scores showed that compositions written in their first language had decreased in quality.
— Eighty-three per cent of parents indicated that they could not communicate with their children in English.
— Students who entered Canada when they were between 12 and 15 years old outscored those who were both younger and older on entry.
— Students who spend more than three years in ESL classes achieve significantly lower grades than those who leave within three years.
— Students report that the most difficult issue for them is meeting native-English-speaking Canadian-born students.
— Older students report that culture shock is a serious problem for them.
— The number of years of schooling received before entering Canada affects students' achievement more directly than the study of English.

First Days

Compared to other parts of Canada, the province of Nova Scotia does not receive many immigrants. Still, the Department of Education is sensitive to the feelings and emotions of newcomers. "The first days in a totally new school environment are particularly crucial for the ESL student. This student may have no English, or perhaps understands only a very few words and phrases in this new language. She may have never been in a school before, and does not know much about her new community yet. She is now separated from those she depends upon for love and protection. Nothing makes any sense to her in this place, and she is feeling lost and absolutely helpless."

Because of this, the department sends a strong message to teachers: "Your responsibility is great in this situation. There are many things that can be done which will smooth the transition for your new student, both socially and academically."

In its *Bilingual Support Service Handbook,* the East Sussex County Council notes: "Children learn best in happy and relaxed surroundings and need to feel part of the class and school right from the start. Appoint a friendly and sensible child to look after the new pupil. If you are given notice of the new child's arrival, explain to the rest of the class what language the new child speaks, and where s/he comes from (another country, another town)."

The handbook also notes that schools can do many other things to help new arrivals adjust: "Try to make sure there are books, pictures, etc. that reflect positive images and his/her experiences available in the classroom. These should not be specially displayed, but should be available as normal classroom resources, to be used by the whole class. It may be helpful if a parent is able to stay at school in the beginning.... Make sure playtime is a happy time—arrange for new children to receive support from other children or adults. At lunchtime, check that any special dietary needs are being catered for, and that children are accompanied at first and shown the lunchtime routine."

Schools that make an effort to welcome ESL students and ensure that their needs are met reap rich rewards. In a newsletter article, Else Hamayan and Ron Perlman pointed out that students who complete ESL programs have much to contribute to the school and the community: "They can teach others their language and about their language; they can teach others about their cultural heritage and their way of doing things. Language minority students can serve as native-language tutors to peers or younger students who need native-language support. They also can serve as links to parents who are not proficient in English. In short, they can expand a school's horizons and open a pathway to all corners of a school building, the community in which the school resides and other lands beyond the school's immediate surroundings. By adopting this view, we would be ensuring a higher likelihood of language minority students becoming proficient in English and succeeding in the mainstream, at the same time providing all students with a richer and more vibrant education."

· · · · · · · · · · · · · · 4

TEACHERS

> Teaching English to speakers of other languages is a distinctive and identifiable area of knowledge that is concerned with the educational and linguistic development of non-English-speaking-background students. It is essential that decisions about their educational program be properly informed and involve suitably qualified TESOL-trained teachers and administrators.
>
> *The Education of Students from Non-English-Speaking Backgrounds*
> Australian Council of TESOL Associations

In 1969, I visited a secondary school to observe an ESL student teacher completing her practicum. The principal, who had once been my principal, called me into his office. "Mary," he said, in a tone indicating that bad news was coming, "I hear that you are getting mixed up in ESL." I nodded. "Don't you know," he continued, "that that will ruin your reputation?" Strange as it may seem today, he had a point. Too often at the time, teaching ESL was the last refuge of those who didn't fit elsewhere in the school system. As a result, ESL had developed a bad name.

Fortunately, times were changing. Young teachers, often former ESL students themselves, and those whose social conscience said we must do more for non-English-speaking children, whether immigrants, refugees or those born in Canada, were taking training and speaking out. Courses, programs, diplomas and graduate degrees slowly developed and were slowly accepted by school systems.

At my university in 1969, just one course in ESL education—Education 478: Teaching English as a Second Language—was available, and I was the only instructor. In fact, the students and I were assigned to a basement room with no windows. Why? Because the administrators didn't think anyone would sign up! Twenty-seven students ended up crowding into that room, which would comfortably have held only 15.

That same university now has six full-time professors and various sessional lecturers to serve students seeking a diploma, a Bachelor's or Master's degree, or a PhD in ESL. This story has been repeated at many universities in Canada, Australia, the United States and England.

Only teachers trained and qualified to teach ESL should be assigned responsibility for teaching non-English-speaking children and adolescents. In too many jurisdictions, ESL is considered part of special education, though this situation is gradually changing. The two fields do share some common features, of course, but it is a mistake to assume that a trained special education teacher is automatically qualified to teach ESL.

Alberta Education wrote: "ESL students' experiences, values and expectations may be different from those of the teacher and their English-speaking peers. It is therefore necessary for teachers to understand the linguistic, social, cultural and psychological implications for students learning English as a second language."

Excellent pre-service training for ESL teachers is a critical component of high-quality programs. Equally important, though, are the personal characteristics student teachers bring to their training. These include patience, sensitivity and flexibility, a flare for organization and innovation, the ability to work independently and to communicate with students, staff and parents, empathy for and interest in students from different linguistic and cultural backgrounds, and a knowledge of a variety of subjects that relate to students' interests.

In my own case, an experience supervising the practicum of one student teacher drove home the importance of these characteristics. When I visited the school where this young woman was practice teaching, the teachers were so dismayed by her incompetence that they questioned why she had ever been admitted to teacher training. I asked them what qualification they considered most important in a student-teacher. "High marks," said one, and the others agreed. They were shocked when told that this particular student had graduated from her university with an A average. Clearly, there is more to effective teaching than the ability to achieve high marks! In the end, I suggested to the student that she find a different vocation.

A document published by the Maine Department of Education contains a letter that Linda Ward Burgess, an experienced ESL teacher, addressed to new ESL teachers. Here is some of what she said:

> You are embarking on a journey in which you will learn at least as much as you teach. You will learn about another culture and you will examine your own culture with new eyes. You will discover new depth in your knowledge of English as the medium of communication in our culture. You will consider just what is important for us to know and how we will know we know it. You will examine what is being taught in our schools and how knowledge is transmitted. You will be challenged to maintain many human relationships and you will reach within yourself to find new levels of creativity and joy in the learning and teaching experience.

College and university teacher-preparation programs must be responsive to the needs of the teachers who will be teaching children and adolescents who are learning English as a second language, and to the language and educational strengths of these students. According to various departments of education in the United States, pre-service training courses should include the following topics, geared to the needs of the children and the aims of the programs for which teachers are being trained: general linguistics, English linguistics, psycholinguistics, sociolinguistics, culture and society, methods and materials, children's literature; bilingualism and theories of bilingual education, theories of second-language acquisition, bilingual and ESL curriculum development, testing and assessing ESL or bilingual students, teaching subject matter through English or the first language or both; cross-cultural counselling, adapting mainstream materials and techniques to ESL programs, developing first-language materials; whole language approach, sheltered English techniques, and involvement with parents and the community. In addition, the programs require that students complete a practicum with a trained ESL teacher.

The qualifications required of ESL teachers vary from country to country and from jurisdiction to jurisdiction within the countries. Some jurisdictions require a certificate, diploma or degree in ESL; others ask no more than teaching experience, on the grounds, presumably, that a teacher is a teacher and any English-speaking teacher can teach ESL. Not so! I have seen too many teachers untrained in ESL methods and lacking any background in linguistics struggling to do what they do not know how to do, and often not knowing what it is they need to know.

To provide a group of teachers with some help in both first- and second-language development, I once visited a Northern British Columbia School with a large population of Aboriginal children who, on entry, spoke very little English. The principal told me to be sure to visit Mrs. Z's Grade 1 classroom because she was a wonderful teacher—95 per cent of the time there was silence in her room. Ouch! This principal clearly had no idea of the qualities required in a knowledgeable and skilled ESL teacher.

In a handbook on educating ESL students, the Massachusetts Department of Education suggested that teachers competent in ESL education be able to do the following:

— Demonstrate knowledge of cultures in contact that can lead to cultural isolation, racial hostility and social isolation.
— Demonstrate knowledge of instructional and curricular techniques and program strategies and models that promote the social and cultural value of students from diverse cultural, racial and linguistic backgrounds.
— Apply theories and knowledge of learning processes relating to first- and second-language acquisition.
— Understand their own ethnic, historical and cultural background.
— Demonstrate knowledge of curriculum, teaching strategies and organizational models for providing dual language instruction.
— Demonstrate knowledge of intercultural relations and communication to create a positive classroom environment for non-native speakers of English.
— Develop and modify curriculum.

In a discussion paper presented at a 1994 TESOL conference in Australia, Susan Hogan suggested that developing professional standards would be beneficial. Doing so would establish expectations, both within the profession and in the public eye, about what competent professionals should know and be able to do. It would also provide a framework for recognizing teachers' qualifications, help create consistent standards for educating teachers and governing entry into the profession, and influence funding bodies.

In-Service Training

Although pre-service training is essential, it is not enough. New research developments that affect teaching practice, changes in immigration patterns that alter the makeup of the student population, and improvements in perceptions of ESL teachers and teaching mean that ESL is a constantly changing field. To stay abreast of the changes, some jurisdictions require administrators, teachers and teachers' aides to take regular in-service training.

For in-service training to be successful, however, it must be tailored to the needs of a particular community or school. This means that staff should be involved in the initial planning. Parachuting in an "expert" who has not taken the trouble to become familiar with the local situation is a recipe for disaster.

Every jurisdiction should be able to call on its own resident experts. The atmosphere at in-service sessions should encourage administrators and teachers to both seek answers to their questions without feeling inadequate and experiment with new methods and techniques. In-service sessions might cover some of the following topics:

— Recent research findings.
— New materials, and how to adapt them.
— Language and content teaching.
— Strategies, skills and techniques used by other teachers.
— Communicating with parents.
— Identifying ESL students.
— Cultural sensitivity.
— Special education and ESL.
— Recent ideas about assessing and placing ESL students.
— Partnership teaching.
— Collaborative learning.
— How to develop reading and writing skills.

In 1992, the state of Illinois started requiring school districts to plan annual in-service sessions for trained and untrained teachers working with ESL students. School districts there must also provide new ESL teachers with training in the specific identification and assessment procedures used in their district, in instructional techniques for working with ESL students, and in program design.

Los Angeles has instituted an innovative staff development program. Every school is required to appoint one teacher from its ESL department to act as a professional development resource. To ensure that this teacher is available to attend regularly scheduled in-service sessions, a substitute teacher is hired for the day. This program enables the selected teacher to assume a leadership role, bring new information and materials to the school's ESL department, share expertise and play a role in solving common curricular and instructional problems.

It's important to note that in-service training programs in ESL should not be limited to the ESL community. To help mainstream teachers and administrators provide appropriate and effective language-support programs and establish realistic expectations of non-English-speaking children, they, too, must be given an opportunity to find out more about ESL programs and how children learn English as a second language.

Other people who come into contact with ESL students, such as custodians, secretaries, teachers' aides, librarians, consultants, counsellors, school nurses, interpreters, home-school liaison workers and volunteers, should also be educated about ESL. They need to be sensitive to students who are likely to need additional patience and understanding, particularly during their early weeks in a school, and to assist in finding ways to help these students. Elected officials should also be informed about aspects of ESL teaching and learning that will help them make wise decisions, particularly about program funding, program types and hiring practices. Because the active support and participation of the school principal is also important in developing effective in-service programs, principals must be well-informed about the three Ps of ESL—policies, programs and practices.

Accreditation

As the field of ESL has matured, professional organizations and education authorities in various jurisdictions have grappled with the issue of whether ESL teachers should be certified. Much of the debate has focused on who should be responsible for establishing professional standards and issuing certificates. Those who teach ESL to adults have led the way in establishing standards, and it is my hope that their efforts will influence developments in the certification of those who teach children and adolescents. Formal accreditation requirements will not only garner ESL teaching the respect it deserves, but will also ensure that the quality of teaching continues to improve.

In an address to delegates to the National Language and Literacy Institute of Australia Language Expo '94, Judy Colman reminded the audience that enrolling in post-graduate studies provides ESL teachers with opportunities to meet colleagues from other jurisdictions and to develop a common terminology to describe their professional activities and the knowledge that underpins them. "This development," Colman said, "is essential to a mature industry which offers varied career paths to its practitioners." She also pointed out that upgrading professional qualifications improves teachers' bargaining power and opportunities for working overseas.

In the mid-1980s, the professional standards committee of the British Columbia Association of Teachers of English as an Additional Language began developing a certification program for teachers who had upgraded their qualifications beyond the basic requirements. In 1988, this group introduced a four-stage certification process:

Level 1—Entry
A Level 1 certificate, which expires at the end of five years, requires:

— An undergraduate degree from an accredited university, or a three-year teacher-training certificate from a recognized teachers' college.
— A minimum of 100 hours of training in teaching English as a second language, including both theory and practice.

— Submission of a satisfactory practicum performance report and a personal reference letter.

Level 2—Intermediate
In addition to meeting the criteria for the Level 1 certificate, the applicant must have:

— A documented record of successful teaching, including two satisfactory practicum performance reports by supervisors or peers, and two letters of reference or reference forms.
— Completed a minimum of 600 hours of full-time classroom teaching.
— Participated in professional development activities over and above pre-service training in such areas as materials or curriculum development, written publications, presenting workshops, attending conferences or summer institutes, etc.

Level 3—Advanced
In addition to meeting the criteria for the Level 2 certificate, the applicant must have:

— Completed five years of full-time classroom teaching or program supervision in ESL, with a minimum of 600 hours of classroom teaching or program supervision in each of the five years.
— Completed additional undergraduate courses in ESL teaching and related fields in addition to pre-service training.
— Contributed to the field of ESL instruction by serving on committees, sponsoring student teachers, presenting papers at conferences, etc.

Level 4—Master Teaching
In addition to meeting the criteria for the Level 3 certificate, the applicant must have:

— Completed a Master's degree in teaching ESL or a related field.
— Completed a minimum of eight years of full-time classroom teaching, with a minimum of 600 contact hours of classroom teaching or program supervision in each year.

Though ESL organizations in other Canadian provinces and other countries have also introduced certification protocols, no common standards exist. Some jurisdictions issue teaching certificates that list what the holder is trained to teach, while others issue certificates that simply give the holder the right to teach. In some school districts, seniority counts for more than specialist training, a situation that is most common in jurisdictions that have been subjected to cutbacks in educational funding. In many cases, this has meant that teachers with years of teaching experience but no ESL training have bumped younger, highly trained ESL teachers. ESL organizations must continue to lobby for effective teaching for ESL students by fighting for the right of ESL students to be taught by qualified ESL teachers.

Bilingual Teachers

A bilingual teacher is someone who is proficient in both English and the students' first language. We must never forget how important it is for immigrant children to have role models from their home culture. Furthermore, a teacher, teacher's aide or classroom volunteer who speaks their first language may at first be the only staff member with whom new arrivals are able to communicate.

In some jurisdictions, the number of children who speak a particular language is high enough that a bilingual teacher or teacher's aide can be employed to work with the children in their first language, helping them not only to learn English but also to keep up with their academic studies.

The idea of hiring bilingual teachers has sometimes been harshly criticized, however. The critics believe that it is the job of schools to teach ESL students English—and only English.

In *Effective Schooling for Language Minority Students*, a document published by the Ohio Department of Education, Ramon Santiago responded to this criticism. He began by asking, "What can we do for our LEP populations that will contribute to their academic success?" Then, he answered his own question:

> First, we need programs staffed with conscientious, sensitive, well-trained teachers, who understand and accept that they may be underpaid and unheralded, but who

know that they can have a great influence on the future lives of their students; who honestly believe in racial and cultural tolerance; and who can strive to show their students how to survive AND succeed in the American mainstream without demanding that they shed their cultural skins…in short, teachers who can not only tell a phoneme from a phonograph, but who are also conversant with the many ways in which children learn language—or just plain learn. Second, we need programs supported by families who feel good about school….

The raging controversy surrounding bilingual education misses the point when the emphasis is put solely or primarily on learning English. The main function of schools is to EDUCATE, not just to teach English….We are not saying that learning English is not important; what we are saying is that the ultimate test of an educational program is not whether it teaches English, but whether it educates.

Santiago's belief in the value of bilingual education was echoed in a 1995 report prepared by the Liverpool Education Directorate. It said: "The special work of a bilingual instructor is critical at the time when a child is making a major shift in language use in the first year of experience of English for schooling purposes. Access to the home language in the school setting enables the child to access concepts already known in the home language and to develop new concepts in their strongest language."

To ensure that bilingual members of the students' cultural community are available to provide language support, it is important for schools to develop and maintain working relationships with the cultural groups in their community. Searching out qualified—and willing—bilingual staff can be a challenge, however, as the California Department of Education noted in its *Bilingual Education Handbook*. "An effective bilingual program provides instruction in basic skills and content in the student's primary language while English language skills are being developed," the document stated. "Before it can offer such a program, however, a school or district must find enough primary language-competent staff to implement it. Accomplishing this feat, particularly for some of the less common language groups, is very difficult. Communication with the language community in question can yield good contacts. Recruiters can speak with university departments, community colleges, churches and clubs where the target language is spoken. They can also put notices in neighbourhood post offices, markets, and target language newspapers."

Other jurisdictions have taken different approaches to finding bilingual staff. For example, a language support teacher in England wrote to tell me what her school district had done. She said: "In order to attract the invaluable services of bilingual colleagues, a few Asian teachers have been appointed as language instructors, rather than as fully qualified teachers. In most cases, these colleagues had gained Indian or Pakistani teaching qualifications which have not been recognized by the British Department for Education."

Paraprofessionals and volunteers can be used to enrich instruction. To obtain the maximum benefit from the extra person in the classroom, Alberta Education suggests that teachers determine what needs the program will address, compile a list of possible duties for the volunteers, clearly define the role of the volunteers, familiarize volunteers with the school procedures they are expected to follow, ensure there is a working space for the volunteers and a place for resources, and help volunteers feel as if they are contributing members of the staff. In addition, they are advised to stress the importance of reliability and consistency and the need for natural communication with the students. It is also a good idea to arrange times when paraprofessionals, volunteers and teachers can compare notes.

When inviting volunteers to help out in schools, it's important to remember that they may not have set foot in a classroom for years. In addition, there may be vast differences in their skills and experience. Still, they may be eager to contribute and ways must be found to ensure that their contributions are valued. In Nova Scotia, Carol Chandler wrote that volunteers are often used to talk to individual students, read aloud to students, listen to students read, and play games that encourage them to communicate.

Peer tutoring can also be effective—if the tutor has clear instructions about what to do, as well as how to do it and why it should be done.

The Changing Role of ESL Teachers

When I first got "mixed up" in the field, ESL teachers had only one role: to teach 15 or 20 beginning ESL students how to speak English. Many teachers did this behind closed doors. At the time, the mainstream classroom teachers in the school would occasionally ask me in hushed voices: "What goes on in there?" I didn't always want to answer this question, because I knew that what went on was not always laudable. Too often, the students were told something like this: "Copy exactly what the dictionary gives as the meaning(s) of the 20 words on the blackboard."

Fortunately, much has changed since those days. Today's ESL teachers are called on to play many different roles. These roles may vary according to the number of ESL students in the school, the ratio of students to ESL teachers, the attitudes of administrators and classroom teachers towards ESL students and teachers, prevailing pedagogical beliefs, and school policies on multiculturalism and racism.

ESL teachers work in a variety of settings. They may work in a self-contained ESL classroom separate from mainstream English-speaking students. They may also provide support for mainstreamed ESL students, either alongside the teacher in the mainstream classroom or on a withdrawal basis.

The preceding tells us where ESL teachers *are*. Another way of looking at roles is to describe what ESL teachers *do*.

In 1989, Jill Bourne conducted a survey of local education authorities in England and found that ESL support teachers play four roles:

— *Remedial role*: Offer individual assistance to bilingual learners to help them complete their schoolwork, either in the mainstream or in a withdrawal situation.
— *Specialist role*: Understand second-language development and the language demands of classrooms and subjects, and have the pedagogical expertise to intervene in order to enhance the language development of bilingual learners.
— *Catalyst role*: Act as an agent of change, providing a professional development resource to school staff and helping other teachers develop policies and practice across

the curriculum to support bilingual learners within a framework of equal opportunities and anti-racism.
— *Good teacher role*: Are effective class or subject teachers who work co-operatively with colleagues to respond to the language needs of all learners in the classroom.

Partnership Teaching

This approach, which is also called co-operative, collaborative, parallel or team teaching, involves the ESL teacher and the mainstream teacher in a close working relationship. The ESL teacher usually works in the mainstream classroom to support the second-language development of individual pupils by collaborating with the classroom teacher to develop suitable curriculum approaches. In describing the relationship between the two teachers, the British Home Office stated, "(ESL) teachers should work alongside the mainstream teachers preparing a lesson, delivering the lesson and re-evaluating the lesson following delivery."

The rationale for partnership teaching is that all teachers share responsibility for meeting the needs of ESL students. According to the Peel Region Board of Education in Ontario, a successful collaborative relationship between teachers begins with the recognition that integration is a developing and changing process. The teachers plan together, share experiences, communicate openly, consider each other, value individual teaching and learning styles, appreciate the other's expertise, and help and support each other. In addition, they must be flexible—and equipped with a sense of humour.

A sense of humour is a prerequisite. I remember walking into a staffroom at lunchtime one winter's day and encountering three teachers who were working together for the first time. "Well, how's the partnership teaching going?" I asked. They looked at one another and burst out laughing. "If you'd asked us that question yesterday at this time, we would have said 'lousily,'" one of them answered. "But after school we got together and threw our comments, good and bad, onto the table. We found that instead of being honest with one another, we had kept both our anger and our praise to ourselves. Today is a new day and things are going just fine."

A pamphlet produced by the Brent Language Service in London pointed out that, to be effective, teachers working in partnership must devote time to liaison. "Co-operative teaching is where the language support teacher and the class or subject teacher plan together a curriculum and teaching strategies which will take into account the needs of all the pupils in the class. Rather than trying to fit pupils into the learning situation, co-operative teaching works to try to change the learning situation to fit the pupils. It implies equal status and shared responsibility, with lead and supporting roles alternating between the two teachers. Depending on how familiar the teachers are with it, co-operative teaching will require more or less time spent together outside the classroom for planning and evaluation, but co-operative teaching always requires some liaison time."

Partnership teaching enables the partners to share knowledge, expertise and skills, and learn from each other while working together to develop curriculum. To ensure that this approach is effective, however, schools must see to it that those working in partnership are allocated time to set goals for, review and evaluate their partnerships. This means that the needs of teachers working in partnership must be taken into account when resources are allocated. The school must establish structures that support partnership teaching across the curriculum.

The Barking and Dagenham Language Support Service in England noted that the ESL teacher and the subject teacher must reach agreement on a variety of issues *before* they embark on a partnership program. They need to agree on how they will work together, set aims and objectives, decide on the content of lessons, discuss how much liaison time they will need to devote to evaluation and planning, and collaborate on preparing worksheets and materials.

For partnership teaching to be successful, the Redbridge Language Support Service in Essex, England, noted that planning is essential. Before teaching together in the classroom, teachers need to discuss the following points:

— What the term collaborative—or co-operative, partnership or team—teaching means.
— Which pupils the ESL teacher is there to support.
— How each teacher perceives the pupils' needs.

— How the workload and responsibilities can be divided.
— How the teaching can be organized to gain the maximum benefit from having two teachers in the classroom.
— How pupils should be grouped both to ensure that ESL students receive the peer-group support they need and to benefit the class as a whole.
— How ESL students can be used as a valuable resource and how their culture and experience can be included in the classroom program.
— What teaching methods, tasks and activities are most appropriate.
— How students' progress can be assessed.

When specialist staff are based in a school, it is important to use their skills and knowledge to achieve the maximum benefit for students. The National Association for Language Development in the Curriculum in England suggested that this involves ensuring that:

— The deployment of specialist staff matches their job descriptions.
— Mainstream and specialist teachers are considered equal in the eyes of children and other staff.
— Specialist and mainstream teachers have equal access to resources, equipment, money and information.
— There is time for joint review, planning and evaluation.
— Procedures exist for monitoring the overall quality and effectiveness of the way specialists are used.

Effective Schools

What is an effective school? The Ohio Department of Education tried to answer this question by listing seven identifying characteristics—a sense of mission, strong leadership, high expectations of all students and staff, frequent monitoring of student progress, a positive learning climate and opportunities for learning, and the involvement of parents and the community.

I would also like to add that effective schools adapt to meet the needs—academic, social, emotional or remedial—of the children. These schools help every child develop or maintain a feeling of self-worth and attitudes that will lead to personal satisfaction in the school, in the community and, later, in the world of work.

A school cannot be effective, however, without effective teachers. In effective schools, all teachers, regardless of subject area or language-support role, are teachers of English as a first or second language.

Effective teachers are constantly engaged in classroom research. They try out different ways of presenting material, different ways of expanding on and extending learning, and different activities to bring the material to life and make it relevant. Some even write about the results of their research for newsletters and journals so that others may benefit.

Teachers in effective schools are aware of cross-cultural similarities and differences between the majority group and the minority groups in the school, and encourage new arrivals to remain proud of their first language and culture. They also help other teachers and students understand and accept the differences in the school population.

In effective schools, administrators and teachers work as a team. The principal usually plays an important leadership role, providing support and helping to implement new ideas put forward by the staff. From time to time, though, teachers, too, may take the lead in areas of special expertise. It's important to note, however, that both principals and teachers must be prepared to be held accountable for their actions—or lack of action. In an effective school, everyone works hard to make the school effective and to keep it that way.

In an article in *TESOL Matters*, Joan Morley adapted material that had been published years earlier by Harold B. Allen. Both were interested in defining the characteristics of an effective, professional ESL teacher. Morley came up with the following list, which I have abbreviated here:

— Competent preparation leading to a degree in teaching ESL—the hiring of unqualified individuals who lack professional training continues to be a problem of gigantic proportions.
— A love of the English language—for the professional, the language is an entity with a life of its own.
— The critical faculty—professionals must understand why they do things when teaching English.

— The persistent urge to upgrade oneself—the ESL professional is a ready experimenter as well as a constant learner.
— Self-subordination—the truly professional ESL teacher is concerned with teaching English because of an intense desire to be of service to others.
— Readiness to go the extra mile—a willingness to do a little bit more and often a lot more.
— Cultural adaptability—sensitivity to cultural differences and cross-cultural understanding have always been integral features of professionalism.
— Professional citizenship—ESL teachers were once homeless mavericks, almost without identity. This situation led to the creation of various professional organizations.
— A feeling of excitement about one's work—true professionals are excited about their work, their teaching, their study, their writing and their research.

I remember driving home from school late one afternoon. It had been one of those days, and I was consumed by the thought that there must be an easier way to earn a living. Then I did some quick figuring to determine what percentage of the students were really bugging me. The answer I came up with was two per cent! Ninety-eight per cent of the students were great—co-operative and friendly, though not necessarily always living up to their academic potential. Stop whining, Ashworth! I admonished myself. Now, in retirement, I often meet or hear from former students who remind me of the funny things I said or did and how hard I made them work, for which they thank me. It's rewards like this that keep us in teaching—even after retirement!

. . . . 5

PROGRAMS

Ours is an increasingly literate society. People who cannot read or write cannot reach beyond their immediate environment, and they face limited career opportunities in this highly technological era. The ESL/ESD program must provide for the acquisition of literacy skills as well as oral skills.

ESL/ESD Handbook for Elementary Programs
Scarborough Board of Education

In the introduction to this book, I noted that my purpose is to present options, not to make comparisons. As a result, I am not interested in commenting on the range or effectiveness of the specific programs offered in Australia, Canada, England and the United States. I do, however, open this chapter with some general comments on the characteristics of effective programs. I then examine, in general terms, the kinds of programs that are available—and the advantages and disadvantages of each. By sharing this information, I hope to help expand the repertoire of options that can be tailored to suit the needs, interests, abilities and background of ESL students in all jurisdictions.

There is certainly no shortage of program options. In fact, the four countries offer a vast array. Twenty-eight in all! And the array of names used to describe the programs, many of which are very similar, is nearly as vast. For the sake of simplicity, then, I have organized the 28 programs into the following six categories:

— Self-contained programs.
— Withdrawal or pull-out programs.
— Mainstream programs.
— Special programs.
— Out-of-school programs.
— Bilingual programs.

If ESL teachers are to choose the most effective program for the students in their care, it is important to understand that every program has advantages and disadvantages—and to weigh these against the needs of the students. For this reason, I offer my own opinions about the benefits and drawbacks of each program—and rely on you to agree or disagree with me. Keep in mind, also, that the policies in place in specific jurisdictions may determine whether a particular program can be effectively implemented in a particular setting.

It's worth noting that this chapter discusses only the first five program categories listed on the previous page. Bilingual programs are dealt with in a separate chapter, which follows. This is because the first five programs deal only with teaching English as a second language; bilingual programs deal with teaching students' first and second languages.

What Makes a Program Effective?

As discussed in Chapter 2, successfully implementing a particular program in a particular jurisdiction often depends on the policies that are in place. Policies are not, however, the only factor that determines the success of a program.

The school culture is also very important. During the 21 years I spent instructing prospective ESL teachers, I visited many schools that welcome immigrant children in Australia, Canada, England and the United States. Schools with effective ESL programs had a special aura that was evident from the moment I stepped into the building. In the foyer, I might find photographs of children from all parts of the world or pamphlets describing the ESL and other programs. In the office, where a member of a visible minority was often employed as an administrative assistant, a friendly reception awaited me. In the classrooms, children of all ages extended a warm welcome, a sign that they had been eagerly awaiting my arrival so that they could ask me questions on subjects ranging from my job at the university to how they could get to university.

I remember one school, though, where the walls between the foyer and the office were papered with notices. All of them began with Don't …. By the time I reached the office, where neither the administrative assistant nor the principal seemed to know much about the ESL class, I was preoccupied with figuring out how many rules I had already broken and how many more I was likely to break. I spent recess trying to bolster the ESL teacher's sagging morale.

When policies are sound, administrators are supportive, teachers are well-trained and students are eager to learn, ESL programs can be very effective. But how can effectiveness be measured? What criteria can be used as a yardstick? To answer this question, I have drawn not only on material found in reports published by various jurisdictions, but also on what I learned in my years of working in the field. In my view, the criteria can be organized into three defining categories—students' academic success, program aims and outcomes, and the school's commitment to ESL.

STUDENTS' ACADEMIC SUCCESS

Some time ago, it was my pleasure to present a scholarship on behalf of an ESL teachers' organization to a former ESL student who was in her senior year of high school. This young woman had not only earned a place on the school's honour roll, but was also busily engaged in community service. When students succeed academically, the drop-out rate is likely to be low. In addition, academic success often goes hand in hand with social adjustment and emotional well-being. Where ESL students are succeeding academically—and this does not mean that they are all on the honour roll!—we can expect to find a healthy language-learning environment where the first language is regarded as an asset. Well-trained teachers, adequate classroom resources and a library that includes books in minority languages all help improve students' chances of achieving well. Most important, though, are the teacher's expectations. Students who are expected to succeed will succeed.

PROGRAM AIMS AND OUTCOMES

If outcomes are to be evaluated, aims must be made explicit. Regular evaluation by professionals knowledgeable about teaching ESL is an important factor in improving weak areas and building on strengths. The evaluation must determine whether the program's aims are tailored to meet the linguistic, academic, social and affective needs of the students. Good programs do just that.

ESL programs are most effective when everyone in the school feels a sense of ownership of the ESL program. This happens when the entire staff is committed to helping ESL learners and shares a vision of what can be accomplished. The support provided by administrators is also important, as is a continuing commitment to professional development.

Though in some instances, individual schools must decide whether to choose an assimilation or acculturation model for their ESL students, this choice is usually mandated by a higher authority. Assimilation requires students to replace their heritage culture with their new culture. Acculturation produces students who embrace English and the majority culture while continuing to speak their first language and retaining significant aspects of their heritage culture. Because research shows that students benefit both academically and socially when they develop in two languages and two cultures, my own preference is definitely for acculturation.

Self-Contained Programs

The many self-contained programs offered in the four countries have one feature in common: all the students in a class are learning English as a second language. The setting in which they are learning, however, varies considerably:

— *School or district reception centre*: Students new to the country may spend days or weeks at a reception centre where they are assessed to determine the best placement for beginning the process of learning English.
— *Full-day reception class*: For up to a year—and sometimes even longer—students spend all day in the ESL class receiving intensive language training. They may be assigned to classes according to their level of English proficiency.
— *Half-day reception class*: Students spend half the day—morning or afternoon—in the ESL reception class and the other half in a homeroom or subject classes.
— *Transitional or sheltered academic class*: These classes are designed to provide a bridge between the ESL program and academic subject classes. In many cases, an ESL teacher and a subject teacher teach in partnership—un-

less the ESL teacher is fully versed in the subject matter that must be covered before the students are ready to enter mainstream classes.

— *ESL credit class*: These classes, which may be offered in English, math and science, are usually available only to older adolescents. Although not usually recognized as prerequisites for admission to colleges or universities, they may be recognized at colleges that operate upgrading programs for ESL students interested in enrolling in post-secondary education.

An important advantage of self-contained classes is that students receive intensive English-language instruction from an ESL specialist who understands their linguistic, cultural, social and emotional needs. In transitional or sheltered classes, students may benefit when two teachers—the ESL teacher and the subject teacher—analyze their needs and devise activities to meet those needs.

Recent language-learning theories, however, indicate that the total segregation of ESL students may hinder rather than help their progress. Furthermore, there is the risk of these classes becoming something of an ESL ghetto. Unless an attempt is made to integrate ESL students with their English-speaking counterparts for at least some activities during the day, the teacher is their only English-speaking model. This gives them little incentive to use the language they are learning to communicate with others their own age. Furthermore, when placed in self-contained classes, adolescents in particular tend to feel negatively labelled and excluded from regular school life.

Students in transition classes sometimes complain that they are kept in these classes too long; they quickly learn that earning credits is the name of the game in secondary school and are often prepared to risk failure in return for the opportunity to try their wings in a regular credit class.

The teacher is often the key to the success of self-contained programs. If the teacher is untrained or incompetent, students may suffer through a wasted year. Even a highly trained teacher, though, may sometimes be overprotective, delaying students' integration into a mainstream class. Delays can also be caused by mainstream teachers who do not wish to deal with ESL students until they are fluent in English.

Withdrawal or Pull-Out Programs

In these programs, an ESL teacher works with students outside the homeroom or subject class. Withdrawal programs operate in a variety of forms:

— *English language or learning centres*: Students leave their home rooms or subject classes to go to a language or learning centre, where they join other students either of the same age or with the same level of English proficiency. They are taught by an ESL teacher.

— *Itinerant or peripatetic programs*: Students are withdrawn from mainstream classes and instructed by an itinerant or peripatetic ESL teacher, often called an English language support teacher. The time available for instruction often varies, depending on the teacher's workload and the distance between the schools served.

— *Tutorial programs*: Volunteers, such as English-speaking or bilingual parents, grandparents or retired teachers, work with individual students or small groups under the guidance of an ESL teacher.

— *Central resource team programs*: ESL staff at a district office respond to the needs of children when called upon to do so by individual schools.

— *Buddy program*: If possible, the new arrival is paired first with a peer who speaks the same first language and can introduce the student to various aspects of school life. Later, the ESL student is paired with another student who speaks only English. This student helps the ESL learner with schoolwork and extracurricular activities. The pair may work together at the back of the classroom, in the library or elsewhere.

Because recently arrived immigrants sometimes find it difficult to cope emotionally and psychologically when they are introduced to a new school system, withdrawal programs can help them get their bearings away from the pressures of the regular classroom. These programs give students the benefit of one-on-one or small-group language training and offer them an opportunity to ask questions or even complain about some aspects of school life. In addition, a language centre can provide support for mainstream teachers and may become the focal point for multicultural or anti-racist activities within a school.

A drawback of these programs is that students do miss what is happening in the mainstream classroom. Furthermore, too many students are sometimes sent to the centre, or students with behavioural rather than language problems are sent. Both these circumstances can hamper the work of the centre teacher.

Mainstream Programs

In general, ESL students are funnelled into two kinds of mainstream programs:

— *Mainstream—with support*: ESL students are placed in regular mainstream classes. To ensure that they receive the help they need, they are either withdrawn for short periods or the ESL teacher visits them in the classroom and works with the student and the teacher.
— *Mainstream—without support*: ESL students are enrolled in mainstream classes and given no additional help.

Mainstreaming provides ESL students with a variety of English-speaking models. Students who are mainstreamed after spending time in a reception class see the move as an indication of their success in learning the new language and coming to terms with the school culture. Mainstreaming can promote students' self-esteem, provide motivation and satisfy social and emotional needs. It requires students to move from learning the new language to using it, which, of course, assists the learning process. At the same time, mainstreamed ESL students are constantly challenged to try and make sense of the language they hear in the context of the regular classroom. They cannot wait to be taught, but must formulate and test their own hypotheses about how English works.

When they move into the mainstream, many students thrive. Some, however, are mainstreamed too soon, without adequate provision for support. They may find the challenge of learning the new language on their own too difficult, especially if the teacher and class are not sympathetic to or understanding of their difficulties. When students are mainstreamed, it is often assumed that their English proficiency, knowledge of subject matter, and willingness to ask questions equips them to progress smoothly. Unfortunately, this assumption is not always correct. As a result, mainstream programs that offer no further support are often called sink-or-swim programs.

When they find themselves unable to cope, ESL students, who are often under intense pressure at home to do well academically, may see themselves as failures. Fear of failure, fear of ridicule, and loneliness may cause some students to drop out of school.

Special Programs

A variety of special programs have been devised to meet the particular needs of particular children. Here are some:

— *Individual education plans or programs*: In consultation with the student, an ESL teacher or a subject teacher or both records a plan setting out the aspects of English and subject matter the student is expected to master during the coming term. The plan also identifies who is responsible for the various elements of the program.

— *Academic booster programs*: These are designed to help students fill in gaps in their knowledge of specific subject matter.

— *Vocational or pre-employment programs*: These classes may contain both English-speaking and non-English speaking students. Students may spend time training outside the school at a vocation of their choice while learning the language of the vocation in school.

— *Special education programs*: Depending on numbers and the level of need, students with special needs may be placed in a small self-contained special education class or withdrawn for specific periods from an ESL or mainstream class. The teacher may be trained in both special education and ESL, or a special education and an ESL teacher may work in partnership.

— *Programs for the gifted or talented*: Like their gifted or talented English-speaking peers, ESL students with special gifts or talents are placed in a fast-track or enriched program that encourages them to explore topics in greater depth.

— *Basic literacy programs*: These programs are designed for older students who are illiterate in their first language and need help not only in learning to read and write but also in building self-esteem.

— *Programs for students at risk*: Students whose previous or present lifestyle or lack of education places them at risk of failure or of dropping out of school entirely are offered one-on-one counselling and teaching.

— *Study skills programs*: Students who need additional help in learning to use the library, make notes, use the dictionary and thesaurus, draw graphs and so on are provided with assistance.

— *Pre-school programs*: Five- and six-year-old children may be placed directly in an English-speaking kindergarten where they are immersed in English. They may also be placed in a program in which the teacher or teacher's aide is bilingual and can use the children's first language to help them learn English and understand what is expected of them. The children may then enter an English-speaking kindergarten or primary class.

When students are placed appropriately, each program has advantages that enable them to build on their background knowledge while moving forward. This prevents them from experiencing the sense of failure that may occur when they try to bridge an academic or skills gap on their own.

Graduates of vocational programs, for example, may be in a position to claim local experience. They may also have made useful contacts, learned how to conduct an effective job search, and discovered where to seek further training. All these considerations enhance their chances of landing a job.

Special education students, illiterate students with learning problems, and others at risk of failure for any reason may need considerably more help than can be given in a regular classroom. For students who might otherwise drop out of school because of frustrations caused by constant failure and unhappiness, the extra help may mean that they will, in time, be integrated into the mainstream.

Gifted and talented students benefit from being moved on as quickly as possible. Forcing them to wait for peers who may not be progressing as quickly can be frustrating for them and interfere with their chances of achieving success.

By encouraging five- and six-year-olds to learn in both their first language and English, pre-school ESL programs help maximize children's potential.

Unfortunately, special programs also have disadvantages, especially when students are not placed and monitored carefully by sensitive and knowledgeable teachers and administrators. Programs may lack substance and a sense of purpose. When preparing an individual placement plan, for example, consultation between student and teachers is essential if the plan is to reflect the student's needs.

Failure to accurately diagnose ESL students' learning problems can result in the incorrect placement of students in special education classes, which sometimes amount to little more than a convenient dumping ground for children who don't seem to fit anywhere else. Furthermore, if the special education teacher is not trained in both special education and ESL, the children may suffer through a series of dull, meaningless exercises that teach them nothing except to hate school.

Like English-speaking students in some special education classes, students in academic booster programs may end up wearing a "slow learner" label when they may, in fact, be perfectly capable learners who simply need to fill in gaps in their previous education. And, like special education programs, vocational programs can become a convenient place for shunting aside those who really need more language or skills training, an academic booster program or a special education program.

Poor development in both their first and second languages can result when pre-school children are taught by inadequately trained teachers or day-care workers. Furthermore, unless the importance of supporting children's first-language development is carefully explained to parents, they may believe that they must focus exclusively on fostering their child's English proficiency.

Out-of-School Programs

These programs occur after school, on Saturday mornings, or during holidays. They may be organized by the school, the school district, an ethnic or cultural organization, or a group of volunteers eager to help new arrivals. When well-organized and well-operated, these programs help students feel that they are making progress.

— *After-school or Saturday morning classes*: These provide students with additional help in learning English.
— *Homework clubs*: Students get help not only with doing their homework but also in understanding what the homework assignment requires.
— *Summer school programs*: These enable students to continue to acquire English, even during summer vacations when they risk forgetting some of what they have already learned.
— *Writing workshops*: Students focus on various aspects of effective writing.
— *Museum and art programs*: Students are taken to museums and art galleries to learn about the culture they are entering, as well as other cultures, including their own.
— *Family literacy programs*: These are ESL classes for youth who are not attending school, as well as parents.

. . . . 6

BILINGUAL EDUCATION

When schools are active in their promotion of bilingualism they will have a language policy which recognizes the cognitive and academic benefits of bilingualism, celebrates language diversity, links directly with equal opportunities and anti-racism policies, and is applied equally across all areas of the curriculum.

NALDIC *Working Paper 3*
National Association for Language Development
in the Curriculum

Advocates of bilingual education believe that it is unnecessary to abandon a first language in order to learn a second language. What's more, they maintain that keeping up and even improving proficiency in the first language actually enhances the ability to acquire a second language. This belief is rooted in research that suggests that students who are proficient in their first language will acquire English more quickly and easily, and that those who can read in their first language will learn to read faster and more easily in English. As a result, it is neither useful nor practical—and may, in fact, be counterproductive—to encourage parents of ESL students who do not themselves speak English well to try to speak English with their children at home. In a document titled *Educating Iowa's Limited English Proficient Students*, the Iowa Department of Education noted: "Parents can provide much support in the first language and should be encouraged to speak and read to their children in any language that is comfortable for them. The school and the parents together can plan for rich and pleasant experiences for LEP students in English, both in and out of school."

In many cities and small towns in all four countries, as many as 15 different languages may be spoken by the 20 or so students in an ESL class. In parts of the United States, however, and to a far lesser degree in Australia, Canada and England, it is possible to put together a class of non-English speaking students who all speak the same first language. In some jurisdictions where this situation exists, bilingual education programs have been introduced. The programs encourage students to learn in both their first language and English.

Bilingual Programs

Bilingual education is a term that is used to describe four distinct kinds of programs:

— *Transitional programs*: The teacher or teacher's aide—or both—speak the common first language and use it to help students learn English. Once the students have become proficient in English and no longer need explanations in their first language, it is no longer used in the classroom and the students are moved into the mainstream. A bilingual education handbook published by the California Department of Education states: "In effective bilingual programs, the language the child is familiar with from his or her upbringing is used to expand the student's general knowledge of the world and higher-order thinking skills until a command of English is developed sufficiently to allow a transition to the mainstream program."

— *Maintenance or development programs*: Teachers are bilingual and students learn in both languages throughout their schooling. When they graduate, they are fluent and literate in both English and their first language. Besides equipping students with skills that are transferable to English and sending the message that students' first language and culture are valued and respected, the opportunity to continue studying in their first language often means that students will reap economic rewards later in life.

— *Two-way bilingual programs*: These classes are also called two-way language development programs, bilingual immersion programs, or dual language programs. Classes comprise a mix of non-English speaking students who share a first language and are learning English, and English-speaking students who are learning the ESL students' first language. In many cases, the first language is Spanish. The programs are designed to ensure that the non-English-speaking students become literate in both English and their first language, and that the native-English-speakers become proficient in the minority language while making normal progress in English. The performance of both groups is measured against the same standards used to assess mainstream students. Students in these programs generally develop a positive attitude toward both languages and cultures.

— *Bilingual-bicultural programs*: Classroom instruction is carried out in English and the students' first language, but also includes instruction in the history and culture of the host country as well as in customs and values of the cultures associated with the languages being taught.

A guide produced for schools in Portland, Oregon, summarized what bilingual programs do as follows:

— Use students' primary languages as vehicles for learning a second language.
— Involve parents at all stages.
— Develop literacy in the first language.
— Recognize that students' proficiency in the two languages is at different stages of development.
— Use the linguistic, academic and socio-cultural resources of students' home communities as tools to teach academic knowledge and skills.
— Focus on students' linguistic, cognitive-academic and socio-cultural development.
— Provide first-language instruction in areas such as science, mathematics and social studies to develop cognitive-academic concepts.
— Include ESL instruction to develop proficiency in oral and written English.
— Use sheltered English to reduce language barriers to subject matter in English.

In Texas, the Education Code requires schools to address the affective, linguistic and cognitive needs of ESL students. It suggests that these students are more confident when basic concepts relating to the school environment are introduced in their first language and in English because this helps them identify with the history and culture of both languages. Linguistically, they must be instructed in comprehension, speaking, reading and composition in their home language and English. Cognitively, they must be provided with instruction in mathematics, science, health and social studies in their home language and English. Furthermore, instruction in all content areas must ensure that they master content and thinking skills.

To be successful, bilingual education must be carefully designed and implemented. The Portland guide outlines some of the factors to keep in mind when introducing a bilingual program:

— What language groups are in your building?
— What is the history of the targeted population?
— How will you begin the planning?
— How are you planning to involve parents?
— Is the existing staff receptive to bilingual education?
— What is the availability of appropriate staff?
— What is your long-term staffing plan?
— What and how much building space is needed?
— What is the availability of materials in the target language?
— What partnerships can be developed with business and the community?
— How will bilingual education be included in your building's site-based management plan?

As in other areas of education, parents can play a vital role in supporting their children. But they can do this only if teachers and administrators communicate with them and help them feel welcome in the school.

The Debate over Bilingual Programs

In the final years of the 20th century, public debate simmered over the effectiveness of bilingual programs. In 1998, the debate boiled over in California, when voters were asked to approve measures curtailing the practice of teaching children in two languages. The inflammatory language of the preamble to the initiative, known officially as Proposition 227, reflected the strength of the feeling against bilingual education. One of the proposition's clauses, for example, accused California public schools of doing "a poor job of educating immigrant children," and charged that the school system wasted money on "costly experimental language programs whose failure over the past two decades is demonstrated by the current high drop-out rates and low English literacy levels of many immigrant children."

On June 2, 1998, California voters approved Proposition 227, despite the efforts of many in the ESL field to persuade them to vote against it. Though the measure allows some children to continue to enrol in bilingual classes in certain circumstances, it has meant that most non-English-speaking California students are now taught in sheltered English immersion classes for a maximum of a year. Once the year is up, they are transferred to mainstream classrooms, though they may continue to receive English-language tutoring from someone who speaks their first language. To ensure that tutors are available, the state established a program to provide instruction in English to parents or other community members who pledge to provide personal English-language tutoring to ESL students.

California isn't alone in introducing initiatives to cut back on bilingual education, however. The English Language Fluency Act, an amendment to the federal Elementary and Secondary Education Act of 1965, proposes to limit federal funding for bilingual programs to three years. It would also require states that receive federal funding to include ESL students in standardized testing programs and remove the requirement that all states or localities provide bilingual education.

Representing TESOL, the national association of ESL teachers in the United States, Anna Uhl Chamot presented a submission opposing the proposed changes to the House Subcommittee on Early Childhood Education. Chamot pointed out that the changes would prevent local education agencies from making informed educational decisions, imperil the civil rights of children, eliminate the ability of school districts to target services to new immigrants most in need, curtail the development of qualified teachers, and deny children cognitive, academic and economic advantages.

As the debate continues to rage, it is clear that the ESL community must do a more effective job of reaching out and educating the public—and politicians—about the critical importance of encouraging students to continue developing their first-language skills at the same time as they are learning English. This message is reinforced in a TESOL publication titled *ESL Standards for Pre-K-12 Students*. It states: "Effective education for ESOL students includes the maintenance and promotion of ESOL students' native languages in school and community contexts." To back up this statement, the document points out that proficiency in the first language facilitates students' ability to learn a second language, a contention bolstered by research showing that the achievement of second-language learners improves significantly when they are able to use their first language to learn in school. In addition, research shows that ESL students who have the opportunity to learn in both languages tend to stay in school until they graduate. Furthermore, it points out that bilingualism is an asset for the individual and for society.

My own view is that the role of the school is to make children *more* than they were when they entered its doors. But children who arrive at school speaking a language other than English and leave speaking only English have been made *less* than they were.

Heritage Languages

Unlike the United States, Australia, Canada and England have few clusters of speakers of one language. As a result, bilingual education programs in these countries are not as extensive. Instead, classes designed to help children continue to develop their ability to speak their first language are sometimes offered as credit courses with a regular place in the school timetable. It is more common, however, to find these classes being taught after school or on Saturday mornings by members of the various ethnic communities. This may change, however, as more and more languages become accepted as criteria for fulfilling the modern language requirement for graduation from high school and entry to university.

Many jurisdictions in all four countries have drafted statements supporting the idea of encouraging non-English-speaking children to continue speaking their first language. The Greenwich Directorate of Education in England, for example, said that it "respects the basic human right of all people to maintain their languages, as enshrined in the (European Economic Community) regulations and in the Human Rights

Charter. This right should be reflected in the curriculum of all educational institutions, which should seek to promote a positive educational ethos in which a range of languages and dialects can flourish."

Children should be helped to maintain fluency in their first language for many reasons. Heritage language instruction or the use of the heritage language in the classroom:

— Helps students understand and clarify the concepts being taught and the academic language being used.
— Aids their intellectual and cognitive development.
— Promotes their self-esteem.
— Helps them learn English, because skills learned in one language can be transferred to the other language.
— Prepares them for living and working in cross-cultural environments.
— Enables them to talk to senior members of their family, and to other students who speak the same language.
— Facilitates the integration of language and content learning, which enables them to keep up academically while they are learning English.
— Improves their ability to adjust to new environments and modes of thinking and behaving.
— Fosters the feeling that their first language is worthwhile.
— Extends their vocational and life options.
— Enhances their personal and cultural identity.
— Provides support as they make the transition from learning in their first language to learning in English.
— Increases their awareness of cultural diversity.

The Minority Ethnic Curriculum Support Service of Hertfordshire County Council in England summed up these points in a document that stated: "Bilingual people use both their languages as one whole language repertoire, as a set of languages that are internally united. In order to assess the aptitudes and potentials of the pupils and respond to their development needs, their whole language repertoire should be appraised."

CURRICULUM AND METHODS

The pace of change in most areas of life is rapid. As the needs of students change, the programs offered in schools must be adapted to respond to them. The process of curriculum development, implementation, and review, then, does not stop with this document. The process of revision will be ongoing, based on a continuous dialogue among all partners in education.

The Common Curriculum
Ontario Ministry of Education

In the days when the audio-lingual habit approach was the prevalent ESL teaching method, textbooks were full of exercises designed to teach phonology, morphology and syntax. Content was merely a vehicle by which students were taught to master the sounds, word formation patterns and grammar of English. The exercises usually moved from sentence constructions that the textbook writers believed were easy to learn to more difficult constructions, which were not necessarily of use or interest to the students. After practising these drills for about a year, students were placed in mainstream classes in the belief that they knew enough English to hold their own in six or seven different subject areas. In fact, some could—but many couldn't.

Gradually, the realization dawned that the content taught in ESL classes could—and should—be drawn from mainstream curricula in social studies, mathematics, science, language arts, art and so on. In other words, the curriculum for ESL students should be the same as the curriculum taught to English-speaking students of comparable age, with adjustments to take into account their level of English proficiency and their previous educational and life experiences. This approach uses language to teach content and content to teach language.

In jurisdictions where education authorities have mandated a common curriculum, classroom and ESL teachers are responsible for breaking it into bite-sized pieces that ESL students can digest and draw meaning from. Although the curriculum should be broken down so that meaning becomes clear, it should not be watered down to the point where the language and content would insult a three-year-old.

This chapter begins by examining recent documents on curriculum development in Australia, Canada, England and the United States. It then moves on to summarize effective methods of teaching curriculum to ESL students.

Curriculum

AUSTRALIA

Since 1989, the state, territorial and national governments have together produced statements and profiles in eight areas of learning—the arts, health and physical education, mathematics, society and environment, English, languages other than English, science and technology. Statements define each area of learning, outline its essential elements, show what is distinctive about it, and set out a sequence for developing knowledge and skills. Profiles describe the progression of learning typical of students during each year of compulsory schooling.

In 1994, *ESL Scales* was published. It is designed to help teachers measure the progress of students learning English as a second language. The document is divided into eight levels, each comparable to a year of schooling. Each level is broken down into three strands—oral interaction (listening and speaking), reading and responding, and writing. These three strands are further broken down into four organizers—communication, language and cultural understanding, language structures and features, and strategies.

The document states: "The *ESL Scales* relate to the English profile and both describe proficiency in the medium of access to other learning areas. In particular, the *ESL Scales* are designed to heighten awareness of English, how it is used, how it develops and how ESL students may be assisted to develop cognitively, linguistically and affectively in it. ... A major consideration in the development of the *ESL Scales* has been the need to ensure the access of ESL learners to outcomes in the eight profiles (i.e., areas of learning) by setting out a clear learning progression based on the distinct starting, entry and staging points of ESL students."

CANADA

Because education is a provincial responsibility in Canada, each province develops its own curriculum. Ontario, the most populous of the 10 provinces, published *The Common Curriculum: Policies and Outcomes Grades 1-9* in 1995. Two years later, it began publishing a separate document for each subject area under the title *The Ontario Curriculum, Grades 1-8*. The purpose was to "provide a rigorous and challenging curriculum for each grade from Grade 1 to Grade 8. The required knowledge and skills for each grade set high standards and identify what parents and the public can expect children to learn in the schools of Ontario."

The curriculum talks of the need for ESL students to be given time to develop their skills in English before they are assessed by criteria used for other students. "The role of the school is to assist such students to acquire the English skills that will allow them to participate in learning activities on an equal footing with their peers, and to meet the specified expectations."

In 1996, the federal citizenship and immigration department published *Canadian Language Benchmarks*. Designed to be a working document for teachers of adult ESL students, it is also useful to teachers of secondary school ESL students because it sets out what is expected of students in post--secondary ESL courses.

ENGLAND

There are strong demands, particularly from business, that schools prepare students so that they will be ready to enter the job market when they leave school.

In 1995, the Department for Education published *The National Curriculum*, which organizes curricula in 11 subjects— English, history, geography, mathematics, science, design and technology, information technology, modern foreign languages, art, music and physical education. In each subject, the curriculum is divided into four key stages, each of which covers a particular age group. Stage 1 refers to children aged 5 to 7, Stage 2 refers to 7- to 11-year-olds, Stage 3 to 11- to 14-year-olds, and Stage 4 to 14- to 16-year-olds. In each subject and for each stage, the document sets out what pupils should be taught and establishes performance standards.

When it was first released, *The National Curriculum* was criticized because it provided for Welsh-speaking students, but not for ESL students. Teachers were concerned that ESL students would be at a disadvantage when writing the Standard Assessment Tests, which are designed for English speakers. In response to these criticisms, the School Curriculum and Assessment Authority issued a statement that said: "All National Curriculum tests offer adaptations to ensure that pupils learning (English as an additional language) are not disadvantaged. For example, for pupils not yet independent in English, there is a possibility of bilingual support to explain test procedures (where this falls within the normal practice of the school) and the use of bilingual dictionaries in mathematics and science tests."

This statement did not completely silence the criticism, however. People working in the ESL field continue to express reservations about the effectiveness of SATs in measuring the progress of ESL students. In a personal note to me, one consultant wrote: "Teacher assessment and SATs rely heavily on teachers' subjective judgements and we need to be always on our guard to ensure that the process of assessment is fair to pupils of different gender, linguistic, ethnic and social backgrounds and with special educational needs."

UNITED STATES

In 1991, the federal Office of Bilingual Education and Minority Languages Affairs appointed the Center for Applied Linguistics to examine content-ESL programs across the United States. The scope of the study extended from pre-kindergarten through to the end of high school. Three of the report's 17 findings are particularly relevant:

— About 54 per cent of ESL programs across the country had developed specific content-related curricula. Of these, 31 per cent were for science, 28 per cent were for math, and 36 per cent were for social studies.

- Sixty-two per cent of administrators reported that a rapid influx of ESL students motivated the creation of their content-ESL programs. Only 28 per cent indicated that the impetus was a legal mandate.
- Many content-ESL teachers had adopted progressive methods and strategies that were supported by solid research.

Methods

Many factors affect children's ability to master curriculum. Though the most important is effective teaching, other factors that come into play are attendance, punctuality, the amount of encouragement received at home, behaviour, research and study skills, work habits, literacy level, computer literacy and level of fluency in English.

A key element of effective teaching is the method—or methods—chosen. Though guidelines and handbooks published by various jurisdictions often describe a variety of methods, they rarely mandate use of a specific methodology. Because they know the students—their needs, interests, abilities and backgrounds—best, teachers are usually expected to choose the method they believe is likely to be most effective for a specific group or individual in a specific situation.

Although some of the methods, such as the Knowledge Framework, CALLA and Foresee were developed specifically for use with ESL students, approaches, strategies and techniques based on mainstream methods have also been successfully adapted to suit the needs of non-English-speaking students. Although many of the approaches are summarized here, more detailed descriptions can be found in journals and books that focus on ESL, language arts and English methodology. They are also the topics of workshops at conferences and professional development seminars—and, if they are not, they should be!

THE KNOWLEDGE FRAMEWORK

In his 1986 book, *Language and Content*, Bernard A. Mohan of the University of British Columbia wrote: "Language teachers must find ways to help (ESL) students learn the language needed to study subject matter in English, while content teachers must devise strategies to help such students understand content and become more independent learners. The joint task of both these groups of teachers is to provide for understandable communication, cumulative language learning, and the development of academic thinking skills."

The book outlined an approach that offered teachers a new way of integrating the teaching of content and language. The approach, called the knowledge framework, is based on the way knowledge is organized—in a textbook or in a student's mind. This organizational framework shows how information, language and thinking are linked and covers six areas. Three of these—classification and concepts, principles and evaluation—are theoretical and three—description, sequence and choice—are practical.

Six principles underlie the knowledge framework:

— Language is learned through meaningful experiences in social contexts.
— Students' cognitive and academic growth should continue while the second language is developing.
— Thinking skills, language and content are interdependent and are common to all subject areas.
— Key visuals such as diagrams, graphs and timelines are essential elements in bridging the gap between thinking, content and language.
— ESL students have developed a range of thinking and language skills that are commensurate with their chronological age but based upon their experiences in another language and culture.
— Efficient instruction aims to meet several objectives concurrently. Efficient language instruction integrates the building up of subject matter knowledge, thinking and language skills.

To prepare a lesson, the teacher first decides on the specific focus of the topic to be taught, then—keeping in mind the principles set out here—lists the thinking and language skills required to help the students learn. Finally, she chooses the key visuals needed to make meaning clear.

The cognitive academic language learning approach—
CALLA—is designed for use with adolescent ESL students who
are being prepared to participate in mainstream content-area
instruction. Its aim is to help students make the transition
from ESL to the mainstream. "CALLA combines English language development with content-based ESL and with instruction in special learner strategies that will help students understand and remember important concepts...," wrote Anna Uhl
Chamot and J. Michael O'Malley in *The CALLA Handbook*.
"The intent is to introduce vocabulary, structures, and functions in English by using concepts drawn from content areas."

The authors suggest that it's important to help students develop learning strategies for four reasons:

— Mentally active learners are more efficient learners.
— Strategies can be taught.
— Once mastered, learning strategies can be transferred to
new tasks.
— Academic language learning is more effective when
learning strategies are mastered.

The CALLA approach involves instruction in three kinds of
learning strategies—metacognitive (e.g., advance organization, selective attention, self- monitoring and self-evaluation),
cognitive (e.g., identifying resources, grouping, note taking,
summarizing, and deducing and inducing) and social-affective (e.g., questioning to achieve clarification, co- operating, and talking to oneself). The content-based curriculum
is based on authentic subject matter drawn from the mainstream curriculum and English-language development is integrated with content subjects. This recognizes that students
need to practise both the language functions used in academic
communication, such as explaining, informing, describing,
classifying and evaluating, and the language skills needed in
the content classroom, such as listening to explanations, reading for information, participating in academic discussions,
and writing reports.

CALLA lessons are divided into five phases—preparation,
presentation, practice, evaluation and extension. They identify language and content objectives, use techniques designed

to make the content comprehensible, and foster the use of a variety of learning strategies.

The brainchild of Richard Kidd and Brenda Marquardson, Foresee derives from the homophone 4C. The first two Cs stand for communication and cognitive academic language development; the final two for content instruction in the classroom. I suspect that there is also a fortuitous link to the meaning of the word "foresee"—to exercise foresight. Isn't the ability to look ahead and be prepared for what might happen in a lesson—to foresee those wonderful teachable moments that conclude with the eyes of the learners sending that satisfying message "Oh, I see!"—one of the hallmarks of an effective teacher?

In *Secondary Sourcebook for Integrating ESL and Content Instruction Using the Foresee Approach*, Kidd and Marquardson acknowledge their debt to the work of Chamot and O'Malley and describe Foresee as an extension of CALLA. They note that Foresee uses certain instructional procedures that are not included in CALLA and places far greater specific emphasis than CALLA on the level of technique.

Although the Foresee approach encourages teachers to plan activities that immerse students in acquiring language, Kidd and Marquardson also emphasize the need for deliberate, planned instruction in a number of important aspects of language and content.

The approach suggests that unit and lesson planning is based on three cognitive principles:

— Learners are active processors of information, which suggests that they learn more efficiently when presented with stimulating and creative tasks rather than mechanical drills and rote memorization.
— Learning is facilitated when students are able to fit new information into their existing knowledge and experiential background.
— Students can comprehend new material either by bringing to bear their previous knowledge (called top-down processing) or by carefully decoding the linguistic message, vocabulary, structures and style (called bottom-up processing).

In their book, Kidd and Marquardson make a statement that is pertinent not only to Foresee but also to all teaching: "Good teaching also involves the ability to assess what students know and are able to do on their own, to estimate what they could know and could do with proper pedagogical guidance, and to assist them to traverse the gap."

The theoretical foundation of Foresee involves three components—content (skills, knowledge and appreciation), language (functions, such as concepts, forms and names, linguistic knowledge, such as vocabulary, structures and discourse features, and skills, such as listening, speaking, reading and writing) and learning strategies (metacognitive, cognitive and social-affective strategies).

When applied in the classroom, Foresee unites theory with practice in the selection of materials and specific instructional procedures. One of its advantages is that it enables an ESL teacher and a subject teacher to work co-operatively on a lesson. The ESL teacher prepares content-based language instruction, while the subject teacher prepares language-sensitive content instruction. These are two sides of the same coin. Teachers soon recognize that Foresee techniques help not only ESL students but also non-ESL students.

WHOLE LANGUAGE APPROACH

The whole language approach is based on the philosophy that language acquisition, whether written or oral, is a natural developmental process. This approach is used in both language and content-area instruction in bilingual, ESL and mainstream English settings. Lessons that apply whole-language principles move from the whole to the particular, are learner-centred, promote social interaction, include instruction in reading, writing, speaking and listening, and reflect the teacher's confidence in the students' abilities.

NATURAL APPROACH

This approach uses language for communicative purposes rather than as an object of formal analysis. The language is acquired in a context as similar as possible to that in which the first language was acquired, through "comprehensible input" provided in a low-anxiety setting. The concept of comprehensible input means that messages conveyed by teachers in the new language are easily understood because they are embedded in an understandable context. They refer to concrete situations and build on the child's knowledge of the language.

LANGUAGE EXPERIENCE APPROACH

This approach involves student and teacher in sharing and discussing an experience. The experience might involve an activity such as cooking, role playing or a game, book, story, personal narrative, film or video.

Once the activity is over, the teacher elicits an oral description of the activity from individuals or the group. As the students dictate the description, the teacher writes their words on the chalkboard or chart paper for all to see. He tries to use the students' exact words, although some subtle corrections may be necessary to ensure that the language is basically standard English. Periodically, the teacher reads back the dictation and encourages students to suggest improvements. Once this phase is finished, the students copy the story for use in follow-up activities.

Developed in mainstream classrooms, this approach has many advantages for ESL students of all ages. They learn, for example, that what they say is important enough to be transcribed. By watching as their spoken words are translated into print, they learn how English is encoded. And when they complete the related follow-up activities, which investigate structures and vocabulary, letter-sound correspondence and spelling patterns, they are doing so with familiar language.

SHARED BOOK EXPERIENCE

Shared reading involves the teacher in reading aloud to students, an activity that is important for both mainstream and ESL students. If the teacher is enthusiastic about reading, students will associate reading with pleasant moments and be motivated to read for pleasure themselves. They will also learn new vocabulary and structures in a meaningful context. The reading selections can be chosen from books the teacher likes, those that suit the students' interests or those that represent their cultural backgrounds as well as other cultures in the community.

TOTAL PHYSICAL RESPONSE

This approach introduces new language through a series of commands to act out an event. The teacher says the commands and acts them out to ensure that the students understand what is expected. The students respond to the commands with appropriate actions. Performing these actions helps students internalize the meaning of the commands. At first, students are expected to respond only physically. They do not repeat the commands or respond to them orally. As they become more proficient, however, they are given an opportunity to give commands to their classmates.

INTERDISCIPLINARY OR THEMATIC LEARNING

Suitable for students of all grade levels, this approach involves integrating related topics of study from more than one subject area to create themes or interdisciplinary units. These enable students to learn language skills and critical or higher-order thinking skills. Interdisciplinary learning is a top-down, meaning-based approach that engages students first in making meaning, then in using language for purposeful self-expression.

CO-OPERATIVE LEARNING

This is an instructional approach in which students explore new topics in small heterogeneous ability groups. Together, the students negotiate meaning by exchanging knowledge and experiences, including the experience of using a second language.

THE COMMUNICATIVE APPROACH

The goal of this approach is to develop interpersonal communication skills by emphasizing the conventional relationships between the forms and structures of the new language and their social or functional purposes. Teaching activities are organized around communicative functions such as making requests and asking permission. These functions are important aspects of classroom interaction that may not be stated as objectives in mainstream classrooms. Nevertheless, they represent expected behaviours that may need to be specifically taught to learners from different language and cultural backgrounds.

Education authorities in Bradford, England, provided schools with an opportunity to develop whole-school approaches to various aspects of literacy. Between 1995 and 1998, one-third of the city's schools, covering the whole age range, participated in an AIMS project. At least 40 per cent of the students in the participating schools were non-native English speakers and, in some schools, this figure rose as high as 90 per cent.

The aims of the project were to improve three areas of the school system: the teaching of language and literacy, students' achievement in English, and access to the national curriculum.

Every year, participating schools identified their objectives, the language development needs of their bilingual students, and their staff development needs. Here are some of the objectives set by various schools:

— To improve the whole-school approach to teaching reading.
— To raise achievement in reading.
— To inspire high-quality creative writing through the use of both Urdu and English poetry.
— To improve the English of pupils and parents through the increased involvement of parents in educational activities.

In 1998, Bernard Campbell and Christine Halsall described the project in a report titled *Lessons in Literacy: Case Studies of Successful Strategies for Raising Achievement in Multilingual Schools*. "Plans are based on an analysis of pupil, teacher and school development needs," they wrote. "Development activities are led well by teachers with good specialist knowledge and staff are systematically involved in trying out new methods and systems. Collaborative, action-research methods are used to trial, observe and evaluate teaching and learning."

When a project is complete, Bradford Education publishes a report on it so that other schools may benefit. For example, Westbourne First School's AIM project involved developing bilingual children's use of language by exposing them to original works of art. Three teachers, Sharon Hogan, Farhat Aziz and Shelley Fingret, worked with Claire Ackroyd of Cartwright Hall Art Gallery on the project, called Miss, They Might Be Stars. Their objectives were to:

— Develop a structure for teachers and pupils to use when responding to and evaluating works of art.
— Explore the ways of extending and reinforcing language after the initial viewing of a work of art.
— Value the interaction of language and literacy, with visual literacy.
— Find effective ways of using both European and Asian works of art in the collections of Bradford Art Galleries and Museums.

Each teacher took a group of students, some as young as four years old, to the art gallery for a half-day visit. As the students viewed a work, the teachers used Rod Taylor's model involving content, form, process and mood to ask questions such as:

— What can you see in this picture?
— What shapes can you see?
— What did the artist use to paint this picture?
— What are the differences between the two people in the painting?

Visiting the gallery to view original works of art was inspiring for the children and sparked a great deal of discussion and language development. This helped foster the children's confidence in speaking and increased their vocabulary. When the project was evaluated, it was found to have met its objectives and more.

Specific Learning Strategies

The following learning strategies are often used with ESL students in conjunction with various methods:

— *Directed reading-thinking activity* (DRTA): To improve students' ability to predict when reading, the teacher selects a passage for the students to read, divides it into chunks and asks the students set questions as they finish reading each chunk: What do you think this story is about? What do you think will happen next? Why do you think so?

— *Advance organizers*: Outlines, key visuals, charts or summaries help students predict the information they are likely to encounter when reading a selected passage.

— *Semantic mapping*: Before reading a selection on a subject such as bears, the teacher writes the word "bears" in the middle of the chalkboard. Students draw on their previous knowledge of bears to provide information that the teacher uses to create a web or semantic map.

— *Peer editing*: Students work together to give and receive feedback on each other's written work.

— *K-W-L*: Before reading, students work with the teacher to record what they *K*now about a selected topic and what they *W*ant to know. After reading, they discuss what they have *L*earned and how this compares to the information recorded before reading.

— *Literary clubs, homework clubs and lunchtime language clubs*: These are opportunities for students to get together, perhaps with native speakers of English, to discuss matters of importance to them.

— *Computer-assisted language learning*: This is becoming more important as schools purchase more equipment and teachers become proficient in using the computer as a tool for teaching language.

— *Key visuals*: Visuals of any kind—films, film strips, posters and artefacts—can inspire discussion and writing.

— *Music*: Singing and chanting in groups provides children with non-threatening, enjoyable opportunities to use English.

— *Volunteers*: Whether they are adults or peers, volunteers can provide valuable one-on-one experiences in reading, writing, speaking and listening

— *Drama, readers' theatre and role playing*: These techniques provide insights into the majority culture, but students need to see others in action before they can copy speech, movement and gestures.

— *Field trips*: These open up local opportunities in work and play and can be doubly valuable if ESL students' parents accompany their children.

— *Journal writing*: Journal writing provides a chance for students to write something every day and receive feedback from the teacher. The topics selected may be personal or related to local or world news.

— *Brainstorming*: A topic is selected and everyone contributes ideas, which are listed by the teacher. At this stage, it's important to welcome all contributions. No idea is wrong.

— *Outlining*: Information is organized to produce an outline, which can become the basis for an essay.

— *Interviewing*: Interviews may be one on one, or the class may interview a visitor. Questions are worked out before the interview takes place.

— *Jigsaw activities*: Individual members of a small group are given or search out pieces of information needed by the whole group to solve a problem or complete a learning task. The pieces are assembled during a group discussion session.

— *Language across the curriculum*: All teachers of ESL students should be aware of the linguistic demands of their subject area and make these explicit to the students.

Selecting Textbooks

Many textbooks are available at a variety of levels and in a variety of subject areas, but not all are suitable. When reviewing textbooks for possible use with ESL students, check the following features:

— Scope and sequence.
— Appropriateness to students' age and grade level.
— Clarity of text.
— Use of visuals.
— New information provided.
— Opportunities for working in pairs or small groups.
— Questions and activities that advance students' cognitive development.
— Opportunities to teach the required features of the ESL curriculum.

Even if a textbook meets all these criteria, the language or content—or both—often needs to be adapted for some students.

A document published by Manitoba Education and Training suggests that content adaptations may include modifying the presentation of material, reducing the amount of material presented, rewording the material using more appropriate vocabulary, and simplifying charts, diagrams and examples, while maintaining the key points.

. . . . 8

PARENTS AND COMMUNITIES

The academic and linguistic growth of ESL students is significantly increased when parents see themselves, and are seen by the school staff, as co-educators of their children along with the school. Schools should therefore actively seek to establish a collaborative relationship with minority parents that encourages them to participate with the school in promoting their children's academic progress.

Report of the External Review Team
on the Vancouver School Board's ESL Programs
N.M. Ashworth, J. Cummins & J. Handscombe

Do you remember your first day at school? I remember mine—I cried all day! Or perhaps you have a memory of your first day at a new school? I remember this, too—I tried to pretend I wasn't there! Do you remember all the questions your parents asked when you arrived home? After one day, how could anyone possibly have all the answers! But still parents asked. It was the only way they could find out what was happening to their child because, until very recently, handbooks that explained things to parents were virtually unheard of. But what a helpful innovation they are—for all parents!

For the parents of ESL students, though, a handbook is not just helpful. It's a necessity. From various jurisdictions in all four countries, I received a variety of handbooks. Many of them are called welcome packets for parents, and most are published in English as well as in the languages of the children who attend the schools. All contain a wealth of information on a variety of topics, including:

— ESL or bilingual education services available in the school.
— How the school system works—basic school program and requirements for diplomas and graduation.
— Curriculum.
— Moving from one grade to the next.

— Testing, reporting procedures and semester grading periods.
— School hours and attendance expectations.
— Counselling services.
— Parent-teacher organization and suggestions for communicating with teachers or the school.
— Extra-curricular activities.
— Immunization programs.
— Transportation to and from school.
— Map showing the location of the school.

The Toronto Board of Education prepares a separate handbook for parents of kindergarten children. It sets out the goals of the program, explains how parents can prepare the child for school, and includes photographs showing what goes on in a kindergarten class—and an explanation of why.

What Parents Want to Know

Even the most extensive welcome packets don't always meet the needs of the parents, though. A 1998 survey of ESL parents in Queensland, Australia, indicated that in the weeks following their child's enrolment, they wanted more information on a variety of topics—the subjects being taught, the value system of the school, assessment methods, reporting procedures, parent-teacher interviews, homework expectations, discipline practices and behaviour management, the rights of parents, the roles of support staff and visiting staff, extracurricular activities, such as excursions and camping programs, and methods of communicating with the school.

A survey of the parents of ESL children conducted in 1993 by the British Columbia Teachers' Federation revealed the following:

— Parents frequently felt that curriculum materials available to their children were inadequate.
— They were concerned about issues of segregation and racism.
— Most expressed concern over funding cuts.
— Some felt that more literacy classes were needed to support students whose schooling had been disrupted.

- They wanted to know how they could help as volunteers—to become involved.
- They expressed concerns about anecdotal reporting.
- They wanted more frequent assessment and evaluation.
- Some criticized the ESL programs, but also said that the provision of ESL classes had greatly helped their children's learning.

To help teachers prepare to respond to parents of ESL children, school authorities in Seattle, Washington, published a list of frequently asked questions. The list included questions like the following:

- Why was my child recommended for placement in a bilingual program?
- What kind of instruction is offered at a bilingual centre?
- What kind of transportation is available?
- Does my child have to go to a transitional bilingual education centre school?
- Is there someone I can talk to about my child's school assessment?

Alberta Education also prepared a list that included questions such as:

- How much does it cost to send my child to school?
- What is the purpose of parent-teacher-student interviews?
- How can I help the school assess and place my child?
- Why is ESL support provided?
- What are the benefits of placing the child in the regular classroom?
- How long will it take my child to learn English?
- Should I speak my first language at home?
- How can I help my child learn English?
- What can I do to help my child at school?

Questions such as these make it obvious that parents new to a school are hungry for information about what their child's schooling will involve. In Maine, the Department of Education suggests that parents be told how long it takes children to master basic interpersonal communication skills and cognitive academic language proficiency so that their expectations of the instructional program and their child are realistic. This kind of information also helps them advocate more effectively for their children.

Communication Barriers

Schools must be sensitive to the issues facing immigrant parents and recognize that communicating with them effectively involves a number of challenges. In 1998, the Queensland Department of Education published a report titled *Overcoming Barriers for Parents*. It outlined factors that may prevent parents from becoming involved in schools:

— Language—where English is not the parents' main language.
— Feelings of apprehension and insecurity in dealing with perceived education "experts."
— Lack of information about and familiarity with school practices, procedures and expectations.
— Inadequate information about the rights of parents with respect to their child's schooling.
— Insufficient options—or inadequate communication of options—available for becoming involved in the school.
— Different cultural expectations of and ways of valuing education.
— Transportation and child care issues.

The same report noted that schools may also unwittingly throw up barriers that inhibit parental involvement:

— The education system may be unfamiliar, threatening or inaccessible to people from diverse linguistic and cultural backgrounds.
— Strategies for promoting effective communication in languages other than English may be in short supply.
— Appropriate protocols for making contact and maintaining productive relationships with communities may not be in place.
— Schools may be unaware of cultural factors that affect communities with diverse linguistic and cultural backgrounds.
— Staff may feel apprehensive when dealing with people from unfamiliar cultural and linguistic backgrounds.

"(Parents of ESL students) have the same hopes and dreams for their children as mainstream parents and families," noted a handbook published by the Iowa Department of Education. "Their frustration comes from not being able to find ways of assisting their children and from being discouraged by the schools when they try to do so. The truth of the matter is they simply don't know what to do. We need parents who are comfortable in schools and knowledgeable about the process of schooling. We must empower parents to take their rightful place along with teachers and administrators in providing a meaningful education for their children."

Something as fundamental as the lack of a proficient interpreter can interfere with communication. Siblings or peers, for example, should be used as interpreters only in social situations. Calling on them to interpret is not a good idea if the matter to be discussed is in any way personal or confidential. The Minnesota Department of Education suggested that teachers, counsellors and administrators can take steps to ensure that the interpretation process runs smoothly. These steps might include:

— Meeting the interpreter ahead of time to explain the purpose and process of the forthcoming activity.
— Explaining specialized and school vocabulary and acronyms.
— Avoiding excessive use of slang and jargon.
— Trying to keep sentences as short and simple as possible.
— Speaking clearly.
— Pausing every few seconds to enable the interpreter to translate.
— Addressing remarks to the parents, family or student rather than the interpreter (e.g., saying, "What do you think about…" rather than "Ask them what they think about…").
— Making time afterwards to discuss the interview with the interpreter.
— Trying to appreciate how difficult interpreting—and using an interpreter—is.

It's worth noting that, during the interview, the interpreter's task is to translate what is being said. The interpreter's opinions should be expressed only once the interview is over and the interviewer and interpreter are alone.

Because the first meeting between teacher and parents is so important, Alberta Education advised teachers to prepare by:

— Ensuring that they can correctly pronounce the student's name.
— Knowing the geographical location of the student's homeland and being aware of some of the political, social and religious features of the culture.
— Understanding and respecting the importance of maintaining the first language in the home.
— Respecting the right of the family to maintain as many of their cultural traditions as they choose.
— Understanding that the parents of ESL students may be going through culture shock.
— Being aware that schools in the host country may be very different from those the parents are familiar with.

Alberta Education also pointed out that teachers can help parents feel at ease during the interview by:

— Being warm and sincere.
— Discussing the student's progress in positive terms.
— Bringing examples of the student's work and explaining the learning that is shown.
— Encouraging parents to take an interest in and value the schoolwork their child brings home.
— Encouraging parents to listen to their child reading stories and books.
— Inviting the family to participate in school activities, concerts and festivals.
— Stressing the importance of telling and retelling stories, legends, poems, chants and songs in the child's own language.
— Encouraging parents to read regularly to their child in their first language.
— Acknowledging the role of maintaining the family's language and cultural traditions in boosting the student's self-esteem.
— Making the parents aware that their attitudes toward the dominant society, school and language play a critical role in determining the child's success.
— Encouraging the family to explore and participate in as many aspects of community life as possible to help en-

sure that their child's educational experience is successful.

— Explaining the importance of learning English themselves in order to participate in life with their child.

Continuing Communication

First impressions are certainly important, but it is just as important to maintain effective lines of communication with parents throughout the school year. Bilingual home-school or liaison workers can help do this. They can help school staff confer, counsel and consult with parents to help them understand what is happening in the school and how they can help meet their child's needs.

Bilingual workers can also help head off the problems and misunderstandings that can arise when parents are unfamiliar with the system. Parents from some cultures, for example, expect the school to make all the decisions about their child's education. But school officials in most English-speaking countries expect parents—and students—to participate in the decision making. A bilingual liaison worker can help resolve such conflicts in expectations.

Other parents may want to know things like whether they have the right to visit the class in which their child is enrolled, whether they can ask why their child is enrolled in a particular program, or whether they can withdraw the child from a program they consider unsatisfactory. Bilingual workers can help answer these questions. But when parents don't understand the long-term benefits of a particular program, they may pressure the school to move the child out of the program too early. A bilingual worker can help explain why the child isn't ready.

In the British Columbia Teachers' Federation survey mentioned earlier, parents said that they wanted to be informed quickly when a problem arose, whether this was behavioural or academic. They also wanted to be kept informed about their child's progress through the various levels of ESL instruction. Some parents felt that report cards were not honest or clear enough. They did not like educational jargon and wanted teachers to be more direct. One strong comment suggested that current report cards were "poison wrapped in sugar."

Collaboration between Parents and School

In a report titled *Effective Schooling for Language Minority Students*, the Ohio Department of Education pointed out the need for "programs supported by families who feel good about school; who have been properly informed about the pros and cons of the various programmatic options available in the school; who feel good about themselves culturally; who won't fall into the trap of advising their children to sacrifice their identity for the sake of being successful ...; and who believe that they can be a great asset to their children—both emotionally and educationally—whether they have a first grade or a college education, and whether they are fluent bilinguals or monolingual in their native languages."

Many of the documents published in all four countries commented on the benefits of collaborating with parents and the community. One of the most important of these is the positive relationship between family involvement and a child's academic progress—when teachers and parents collaborate, children's academic performance tends to improve.

Many of the documents also recognized, however, that it is not always easy for parents to collaborate with the school. They often don't have time because they are attending language classes themselves and may be working at more than one job to support their family. Some are reluctant because they believe their English skills aren't good enough to communicate effectively with teachers or other parents and students. Furthermore, the school experiences of some may have been so unpleasant that they don't feel comfortable in the school environment.

Some parents, of course, do have the time and are interested in volunteering, but don't know how to contribute. For others, the idea of volunteering is unfamiliar, and they may need much encouragement to become involved.

Volunteers can take on a variety of jobs, including:

— Accompanying students on a field trip and helping them appreciate the linguistic and cultural value of a community resource.
— Helping students expand their horizons by talking to them about a cultural object or custom.
— Demonstrating a specific skill and inviting questions.

— Preparing classroom materials and resources.

Volunteers might also be asked to teach children a little of their first language. Children are interested in other languages and enjoy being able to speak a few words of a classmate's language. After one such session, one teacher heard a young native-English-speaking boy remark, "I knew people *spoke* other languages, but I thought everybody *thought* in English!"

Pre-school and kindergarten teachers are often delighted to have an extra pair of hands to help prepare materials, and working in the classroom can give parents the opportunity to watch their children in action. Parent-teacher conferences become much more meaningful when both parent and teacher are discussing the same information.

In most schools, an organized parent association of some sort exists, but participating often calls for more courage than some newly arrived parents can muster. To help non-English-speaking parents feel less hesitant, one school in Richmond, British Columbia, created a special group for new parents. At the end of the year, when the ESL parents felt more at ease with their English-speaking counterparts, this group merged with the main organization. The same school also identified English-speaking "buddy" families to provide information and support to newly arrived families. The buddy family specifically invited the new family to school activities.

If no group exists for first-year parents, however, newly arrived parents should be personally invited to attend parent-teacher or parents' group meetings. In one school with a high percentage of ESL students, the staff room is always open to parents. Another school operates a parent surgery—at certain times an interpreter and teacher take telephone calls from parents with questions. Some schools have organized workshops for parents, providing informational materials in the parents' first language.

Sharon Fenton, a teacher in Vancouver, British Columbia, decided to organize a potluck dinner for the families of students in her class. First, though, the students had to learn what a potluck dinner is. Together, she and the students created a web answering the questions who, what, where, when, why and how. The students wrote invitations to their parents, learned the language of introductions, drew up a food chart, and discussed how to set a table. Fenton invited interpreters—and 35 people showed up for dinner. The students made speeches and the parents had an opportunity to talk to Fenton in relaxed circumstances. The event was a huge success.

Resources

If parents are to help their children with schoolwork, they need to know what resources are available in the school and in the community.

More and more school libraries and some classrooms now contain books printed in two languages for students to take home. Some are storybooks, while others are non-fiction. I have come across the occasional resource club, which provides information about where resources are available and, more important, how parents can help their children use them. Parents also need to know about community resources that are available to adults, such as English-as-a-second-language classes and agencies that can help with personal or family difficulties.

Dealing with English-Speaking Parents

Unfortunately, English-speaking parents sometimes feel threatened when a large number of non-English speaking students enter a school. The concern expressed most often is that standards will drop.

The California Department of Education acknowledged this concern and produced a document recommending that schools take steps to deal with it. The document suggested that the concerns "can best be handled by a number of parent meetings with presentations by experts knowledgeable about the rationale, goals, critical features, and evaluation results for bilingual immersion education; by experienced bilingual immersion teachers who can describe the classroom set-up and the interactions of the different groups of children in the class; by parents of children in bilingual immersion programs; and by children in bilingual immersion programs. Also, the meetings may be more beneficial if they are integrated with both parents of language minority and majority students and if there are individuals who can provide the language support necessary for a bilingual meeting."

Communities

Schools do not exist in a vacuum. They are part of a much broader community—and establishing and maintaining productive relationships with this community is essential to their well-being.

One of the most important roles of the community is to supply resources: funds to pay salaries, purchase materials, and build schools; people to act as aides and information sources; materials such as films, pamphlets, posters; sites for field trips such as museums, art galleries and hospitals; and agencies, governmental and non-governmental, that provide information and counselling on matters of personal or family concern.

Resources can be located by surveying the community through telephone calls or personal visits and by establishing a network of people who are knowledgeable about particular resources in the community that may be of interest to students.

The community can also influence education in general and ESL in particular. The passage in California of Proposition 227 (see p. 106) drove home the point that the attitudes, expectations and aspirations of individuals and groups in the community beyond the school can play an important role in determining the future of education in general—and of language teaching in particular. Parents can also influence education, both within the family and as members of groups that decide how funds are allocated, such as parent organizations or school boards that have the power to control funds and pass legislation regulating programs, curriculum and methods.

The relationship between the school and the community is not a one-way street, however. The community benefits when effective ESL programs produce students fluent and literate in two languages. Not only are the career opportunities of these students enhanced, but their ability to communicate with people from other nations enables them to participate more actively in the life of the community.

Many jurisdictions suggest ways for schools to strengthen their relationship with the community. The Queensland Department of Education, for example, suggested that schools could disseminate information about their programs and activities through a column in a local newspaper and by supporting students in activities that take place outside the school. Many community organizations offer services to non-English-speaking clients and the school can play an important role in ensuring that students and their families are informed about the existence of these services.

.... 9

LOOKING AHEAD

> The year 2000—for centuries that monumental, symbolic date has
> stood for the future and what we shall make of it. In a few short
> years that future will be here.
>
> *Megatrends 2000: Ten Directions for the 1990s*
> John Naisbitt & Patricia Aburdene

As I think about what ESL students—and their
teachers—are likely to face in the new millennium, I find myself concerned about three issues. The first is the phenomenon
of cultural nationalism. The second revolves around the necessity of empowering ESL students, and the third involves
the need to build a cohesive vision of the future. Each of these
issues raises important questions that those who are picking
up the torch in the ESL field will need to grapple with.

Cultural Nationalism

Ten years before the turn of the millennium, John Naisbitt and
Patricia Aburdene predicted the current trend toward global
lifestyles and cultural nationalism. In their book, *Megatrends
2000: Ten Directions for the 1990s*, they quoted designer Paloma
Picasso, who said, "The world is becoming more and more
cosmopolitan, and we are all influencing each other." Even as
lifestyles around the world grow inexorably more similar,
however, there are unmistakable signs that a powerful coun-
tertrend is developing. Increasingly, there is a backlash
against uniformity, a desire to assert the uniqueness of one's
culture and language and repudiate outside influences.

With immigration to Australia, Canada, England and the
United States coming from an ever-widening range of coun-

tries, citizens of these English-speaking nations are expressing concern about the effect of these languages and cultures on their own country. Naisbitt and Aburdene wrote: "The more homogeneous our lifestyles become, the more steadfastly we shall cling to deeper values— religion, language, art and literature. As our outer worlds grow more similar, we will increasingly treasure the traditions that spring from within."

There is little doubt that television and the Internet will draw the people of the world closer together on the surface—but these same forces may push people farther apart at a deeper level. To a high degree, English is already the language used to store and retrieve electronic information, and is likely to become even more pervasive. Naisbitt and Aburdene point out, however, that "just as English becomes the universal language, there is a backlash against that same universality. People are insisting on keeping traditional languages and cultures alive." They call this phenomenon cultural nationalism and believe that, when it is challenged or when there is a new opportunity for its expression, it will rise to the surface.

Now that the 21st century is upon us, are we going to fight or accept cultural nationalism? How will our decision affect non-English speaking immigrant children?

Empowering ESL Children

In an article published in *Beyond Multicultural Education: International Perspectives*, James A. Banks wrote: "When students are empowered, they have the ability to influence their personal, social, political and economic worlds. Students need specific knowledge, skills and attitudes in order to have the ability to influence the worlds in which they live. They need knowledge of their social, political and economic worlds, the skills to influence their environments, and humane values that will motivate them to participate in social change to help create a more just society and world."

Teachers influence whether ESL students are empowered or disempowered. Teachers empower students when they acknowledge the value of other cultures and other languages. They disempower students when they make no effort to rethink their own prejudices and stereotypes, but bring these to

140

the classroom for English-speaking students to copy. Teachers can also empower or disempower students to:

— Succeed or fail in school.
— Enter the workforce as equals or inferiors.
— Live in a closed community or in the wider world.
— Retain or lose their heritage language and culture.

In the concluding remarks he wrote for the book *Minority Education: From Shame to Struggle*, Jim Cummins talked of the struggles waged by people around the world. These struggles, he said, are not for power over others, but for the power to decide one's own destiny without encroaching on other people's right to decide theirs. He said, "We are in the middle of the educational part of this struggle—we do not have the power yet to organize minority education in the way the minorities think would be good for their children."

Cummins also wisely pointed out: "...the struggle has to be well informed. It has to be based on an adequate description of the past and present.... It has to be based on a thorough analysis of what happens and why, at both a local and global level.... It has to be based on a deep and profound intellectual and emotional understanding of what happens.... We also need accurate accounts and analyses of ongoing struggles, with shortcomings and successes, to learn from each other...."

Can you describe to yourself and others the struggle currently going on in language-minority education in your school or district, and suggest some remedies?

Developing a Vision

Years ago, A.I.Wittenberg described his vision of education in *The Prime Imperatives: Priorities in Education*

In a free society, the very best education must be accessible to every child. This means two things. It means that the very best education this society has to offer must be available to every child, but, in addition, that this education must measure up to the best education that is or has been available anywhere. Every child must be educated with the care, devotion, and high aims that were once re-

141

served for a few privileged children of noble birth; for every child is of noble birth.

What is your vision for the education of ESL children? How can this vision be transformed into reality?

In 1973 and again in 1985, I drove across Canada searching out programs for ESL children. Since then, I have visited schools in Australia, England and the United States. As a result of these journeys, I have concluded that the well-being of immigrant children, no matter where they come from or which country they now call home, depends on acknowledging that they possess three inalienable rights:

— The right to facility in the official language of the country and in the language of instruction in schools and higher education.
— The right to continue their education beyond the school-leaving age. In particular, students who arrive in their teens must be given hope that they will be able to master English and content—probably a little later than their peers of a similar age—so that their dreams and those of their parents do not die.
— The right to expect that their linguistic, cultural and racial differences will be accepted by their teachers, peers and community and that their decision to retain aspects of their heritage language and culture will be respected.

Who will help their dreams come true? Who will turn vision into reality?

In her contribution to *Multicultural Education and Policy: ESL in the 1990s*, Jean Handscombe wrote: "In the final analysis, however, the key players in any educational setting—teachers and their administrators, students and their parents—must be involved in reaching consensus as to which policies will govern teaching and learning and how those policies will be put into operation."

To teachers, administrators, students and their parents, we must add politicians. But it is imperative that the first four groups—teachers, administrators, students and parents—create and voice their vision for the education of ESL children. It's important to create a vision for politicians to respond to rather than to wait for politicians to take the initiative themselves.

Politicians should not be left to make uninformed guesses about what is needed.

No matter how creative or cohesive a vision is, however, certain practical conditions must be in place before it can be transformed into reality. These conditions are:

— *Funding and accountability*: Funding must be adequate and stable. Funds designated for ESL education must be directed specifically to ESL programs. Because few mainstream teachers are trained to work with ESL students, money must not be dumped into general revenues and used to help reduce the size of mainstream classes. It may be necessary to audit schools to ensure that the funds are used to help the students who generate them.

— *Teacher training and employment*: In most large communities, ESL students have taken their place in mainstream classrooms. As a result, it is important for mainstream teachers to have some familiarity with the needs of ESL students and the teaching of English as a second language. Furthermore, when teachers are assigned to ESL reception classes or pull-out programs, it should be on the basis of their qualifications for teaching ESL, not on seniority. Would an experienced ESL teacher be assigned to teach a senior biology class? I doubt it. Yet in some jurisdictions where layoffs have caused bumping, it is considered acceptable to place a biology (or math, or history, etc.) specialist in charge of an ESL class.

— *Curriculum and methods*: The ESL curriculum is the regular curriculum taught by using language to teach content and content to teach language.

— *Professional development and networks*: Effective professional development provides participants with additional knowledge and new contacts to add to their networks.

— *Research and planning*: Because computers have made collecting data much easier, there is an explosion of research into everything from the effectiveness of programs to characteristics that help students learn a second language. Sound research provides a strong foundation for planning programs that benefit students.

— *Attitude-changing and leadership*: When adults hold discriminatory attitudes, these can translate into discriminatory practices in the community and the schools that are part of the community. Eradicating prejudice within schools requires leadership. It is often surprising what a difference one determined person can make.

How might your vision for the education of language minority children become reality?

As I said at the outset, I do not expect you to agree with all I have said in this book. Still, I hope the information and comments presented have been helpful—and have stimulated thought and discussion. For now, I'll say no more. The future lies in your hands. May you have many happy teaching years.

. . . .

ABBREVIATIONS

ACTA	Australian Council of TESOL Associations Inc.
ATESOL	Association of Teachers of English to Speakers of Other Languages (Australia)
ATESL	Alberta Teachers of English as a Second Language
BCTF	British Columbia Teachers' Federation
BEA	Bilingual Education Act
CAL	Center for Applied Linguistics
CALLA	Cognitive academic language learning approach
CLD	Culturally and linguistically diverse
CMEP	Child Migrant Education Program
DFE	Department for Education
EAL	English as an additional language
EEO	Equal Education Opportunities Act
EFL	English as a foreign language
ESD	Standard English as a second dialect
ESEA	Elementary and Secondary Education Act
ESL	English as a second language
ESOL	English to speakers of other languages
FEP	Fluent English proficient
HEW	Department of Health, Education and Welfare
HLS	Home language survey
HLS	Home language spoken
HMSO	Her Majesty's Stationery Office

IASA	Improving America's Schools Act
ILP	Individual learning/language plan/program
L1	First language
L2	Second language
LAC	Language assessment committee
LEA	Local Education Agency
LEP	Limited English proficient
LOTE	Languages other than English
NALDIC	National Association for Language Development in the Curriculum
NESB	Non-English-speaking background
OBEMLA	Office of Bilingual Education and Minority Languages Affairs
OCR	Office for Civil Rights
OFSTED	Office for Standards in Education
OISE	Ontario Institute for Studies in Education
PLA	Primary language assessment
PSA	Provincial Specialist Association
SAT	Standard Assessment Test
SCAA	School Curriculum and Assessment Authority
TEAL	Teachers of English as an Additional Language
TESL	Teachers of English as a Second Language
TESL	Teaching English as a Second Language
TESOL	Teachers of English to Speakers of Other Languages

CONTRIBUTORS

The following Australian, Canadian, English and American organizations contributed documents on English-as-a-second-language programs for children and adolescents. The fact that a jurisdiction is not listed should not be interpreted as a lack of co-operation, however; it may not have been contacted.

Australia

Association of Teachers of English to Speakers of Other Languages
Australian Council of TESOL Associations Inc.
Australia Literacy Foundation
Catholic Schools, Sydney, New South Wales
Commonwealth of Australia Department of Employment, Education and Training
Education Department of Western Australia
National Centre for English Language Teaching and Research, Macquarie University, Sydney, New South Wales
New South Wales Department of School Education
Queensland Department of Education
South Australia Department of Education, Training and Employment

Tasmania Department of Education
Victoria Department of Education

Canada

Alberta Education
Alberta Teachers of English as a Second Language
Association of Teachers of English as a Second Language of
    Ontario
Board of Education for the City of London, Ontario
British Columbia Ministry of Education
British Columbia Teachers' Federation
British Columbia Teachers' Federation ESL PSA (Provincial
    Specialists' Association)
British Columbia Association of Teachers of English as an
    Additional Language
Burnaby School District, British Columbia
Calgary Board of Education, Alberta
Calgary Roman Catholic Separate Schools, Alberta
Castlegar School District, British Columbia
Citizenship and Immigration Canada
Dartmouth District School Board, Nova Scotia
Edmonton Public Schools, Alberta
English Language Professionals, Inc., Edmonton, Alberta
ESL/ESD Resource Group of Ontario
Faculty of Education, University of Manitoba
Federation of Women Teachers' Associations of Ontario
Government of Newfoundland and Labrador Department
    of Education
Halifax School Board, Nova Scotia
Manitoba Department of Education
Metropolitan Toronto School Board, Ontario
Moncton School District, New Brunswick
Nanaimo School Board, British Columbia
New Brunswick Department of Education
North York Board of Education, Ontario
Nova Scotia Education and Culture
Oakridge Reception and Orientation Centre, Vancouver,
    British Columbia
Ontario Ministry of Education and Training
Open Learning Agency, British Columbia

Peel Region Board of Education, Ontario
Prince Edward Island Department of Education
Prince George School District, British Columbia
Regina School District, Saskatchewan
Richmond School Board, British Columbia
Saint John School Board, New Brunswick
Saskatchewan Department of Education, Training and
    Employment
Scarborough Board of Education, Ontario
Surrey School Board, British Columbia
TESL Manitoba
Toronto Board of Education, Ontario
Toronto Portuguese Parents Association, Ontario
Vancouver School Board, British Columbia
Victoria School District, British Columbia
Winnipeg School District No.1, Manitoba

England

Coleg Normal, Bangor, Wales
Barking and Dagenham Language Support Service
Bolton Language for Achievement Project
Bradford Education—Achievement in Multilingual Schools
    Project
Brent Language Service
Bromley Tuition Support Services
Calderdale Local Education Authority
Cumbria Education Consultancy Services
Department for Education
East Sussex Bilingual Support Service
Greenwich Directorate of Education
Hammersmith and Fulham Support Centre
Havering ESOL Service
Hertfordshire County Council Education Department
Humberside Education Services
Lewisham Education
Liverpool Bilingual Development Service and Consultancy
London Borough of Richmond upon Thames Education
    Department
National Association for Language Development in the
    Curriculum

North Tyneside Education Services
Redbridge Language Support Service
Sandwell Department of Education
School Curriculum and Assessment Authority
Solihull Education Department
South Tyneside Education Department
Surrey Education Services
Tower Hamlets Education Department
Warwickshire Intercultural Curriculum Support Service
Wolverhampton Education Department

United States

Alabama Department of Education
Alabama-Mississippi Teachers of English to Speakers of
    Other Languages
Arizona Department of Education
Arkansas Department of Education
Biloxi Public Schools/Bilingual Education, Mississippi
BW Associates, California
California Department of Education
California Teachers of English to Speakers of Other
    Languages
California Association for Bilingual Education
Center for Applied Linguistics
Chicago Public Schools, Illinois
City University of New York
College of Education and Technology, Eastern New Mexico
    University
Connecticut Department of Education
Delaware Board of Education and Department of Public
    Instruction
Florida Department of Education
Georgia Department of Education
Healdburg Union School District, California
High Point High School, Beltsville, Maryland
Idaho Department of Education
Illinois State Board of Education
Illinois Resource Center
Illinois Teachers of English to Speakers of Other
    Languages/Bilingual Education

Immigration History Research Center, University of
    Minnesota
Indiana Department of Education
Inter-American Magnet School, Chicago, Illinois
Intercultural Center for Research in Education, Arlington,
    Massachusetts
International High School, LaGuardia College, New York,
    New York
Iowa Department of Education
Jefferson Parish Public School System, Louisiana
Kansas State Board of Education
Lennox School District, California
Los Angeles Unified School District, California
Louisiana Department of Education
Louisiana Teachers of English to Speakers of Other
    Languages
Maine Department of Education
Maryland State Department of Education
Massachusetts Department of Education
Michigan Department of Education
Michigan Teachers of English to Speakers of Other
    Languages
Minnesota Department of Education
Mississippi Department of Education
Montana Office of Public Instruction
National Clearinghouse for Bilingual Education
National Center for Research on Cultural Diversity and
    Second Language Learning
New Jersey State Department of Education
New Mexico Department of Education
New York State Teachers of English to Speakers of Other
    Languages
Ohio Department of Education
Oklahoma State Department of Education
Pennsylvania Department of Education
Portland Public Schools, Oregon
Rhode Island Department of Elementary and Secondary
    Education
San Francisco Unified School District, California
Seattle Public Schools, Washington
State Education Department, University of New York
School District of Philadelphia, Pennsylvania

Teachers of English to Speakers of Other Languages
Tennessee State Department of Education
Texas Education Agency
United States Department of Education
Urbana School District, Illinois
Vermont Department of Education
Virginia Department of Education
Washington State Superintendent of Public Instruction
Windsor Union School District, California
Wisconsin Department of Public Instruction

REFERENCES AND RESOURCES

Chapter 1: History, Laws and Policies

Ashworth, N.M. *Children of the Canadian Mosaic: A Brief History to 1950.* Toronto, Ont: OISE Press, 1993.

Briggs, A. *A Social History of England.* New York, N.Y.: Viking Press, 1984.

Brogan, H. *The Penguin History of the United States of America.* New York, N.Y.: Penguin Books, 1985.

Careless, J.M.S. *Canada: A Story of Challenge.* Toronto, Ont.: Macmillan of Canada, 1963.

City of Bradford Metropolitan Council Directorate of Education Services. *Towards Education for All.* Bradford, England: City of Bradford Metropolitan Council, 1987.

Clark, M. *A Short History of Australia.* Ringwood, Vic.: Penguin Australia, 1963. Reprinted 1992.

Degler, C.N. *Out of Our Past: The Forces That Shaped Modern America* (3rd Ed.). New York, N.Y.: Harper Colophon, 1984.

Department of Education and Science. *A Language for Life: The Report of the Committee of Inquiry under the Chairmanship of Sir Alan Bullock* (The Bullock Report). London: HMSO, 1975.

Education for All: The Report of the Committee of Inquiry into the Education of Children from Ethnic Minority Groups (The Swann Report). London, England: HMSO, 1985.

ESL Scales: A Joint Project of the States, Territories and the Commonwealth of Australia Initiated by the Australian Education Council. Carlton, Vic.: Curriculum Corporation, 1994.

Fernandez-Armesto, F. *Millennium: A History of the Last Thousand Years.* New York, N.Y.: Scribner's, 1995.

Grenville, J.A.S. *A History of the World in the Twentieth Century.* Cambridge, Mass.: The Belknap Press of Harvard University Press, 1994.

Johnson, P. *Modern Times: From the Twenties to the Nineties.* New York, N.Y.: HarperCollins, 1991.

Morton, D.M. *A Short History of Canada.* Edmonton, Alta.: Hurtig, 1983.

New South Wales Department of School Education. *Ethnic Affairs Policy Statement Plan, 1993-1997.* Sydney, NSW: New South Wales Department of School Education, 1993.

Office of the Secretary, United States Department of Education. *The Condition of Bilingual Education in the Nation: A Report to the Congress and the President.* Washington, D.C.: United States Department of Education, 1992.

Seattle Public Schools, Department of Transitional Bilingual Education. *Operations Manual.* Seattle, Wash.: Seattle Public Schools, c. 1993-94.

Skutnabb-Kangas, T. & J. Cummins, Eds. *Minority Education: From Shame to Struggle.* Clevedon, Avon: Multilingual Matters, 1988.

South Australia Commonwealth State Migration Committee. *Settlement Plan, South Australia, 1993/1997.* Adelaide, SA: South Australia Government, c. 1992.

Victoria Board of Studies. *ESL Companion to the English CSF.* Melbourne, Vic.: Victoria Board of Studies, 1996.

Chapter 2: The Evolution of Policies

Alberta Education. *Language Education Policy for Alberta.* Edmonton, Alta.: Alberta Education, 1988.

Australian Council of TESOL Associations. *Statement on Accountability in Commonwealth-Funded English as a Second Language Programs in Schools.* School of Education, La Trobe, Vic.: ACTA, 1994.

British Columbia Ministry of Education. *ESL: Policy, Guidelines, and Resources for Teachers.* Victoria, B.C.: British Columbia Ministry of Education, 1999.

Burnaby, B. & A. Cummings, Eds. *Socio-Political Aspects of ESL.* Toronto, Ont.: OISE Press, 1992.

Calgary Board of Education. *Topics—Policies.* Calgary, Alta.: Calgary Board of Education, 1995.

Cumming, A. *A Review of ESL Services in the Vancouver School Board.* Toronto, Ont.: Ontario Institute for Studies in Education, 1995.

Cummins, J. *Negotiating Identities: Education for Empowerment in a Diverse Society.* Ontario, Calif.: California Association for Bilingual Education, 1996.

Education for All: The Report of the Committee of Inquiry into the Education of Children from Ethnic Minority Groups (The Swann Report). London, England: HMSO, 1985.

Egginton, W. & H. Wren, Eds. *Language Policy: Dominant English, Pluralist Challenges.* Canberra, Australia: John Benjamins/Language, 1997.

Esling, J.H., Ed. *Multicultural Education and Policy: ESL in the 1990s.* Toronto, Ont.: OISE Press, 1989.

Herriman, M. & B. Burnaby, Eds. *Language Policies in English-Dominant Countries: Six Case Studies.* Clevedon, Avon: Multilingual Matters, 1996.

Iowa Department of Education. *Educating Iowa's Limited English Proficient Students.* Des Moines, Iowa: Iowa Department of Education, 1996.

Kent County Council. *A Management Summary.* Gravesend, Kent: Kent County Council, 1992.

Martin-Jones, M. "Language Education in the Context of Linguistic Diversity: Differing Orientations in Educational Policy Making in Britain." In *Multicultural Education and Policy: ESL in the 1990s.* J.H. Esling, Ed. Toronto, Ont.: OISE Press, 1989.

Mazerolle, D. Letter to the Author. Moncton, N.B.: District No. 2, 1995.

Ricento, T.K. & N.H. Hornberger. "Unpeeling the Onion: Language Planning and Policy and the ELT Professional." In *TESOL Quarterly.* Vol. 30, no. 3: 1996.

School Curriculum and Assessment Authority. *Teaching English as an Additional Language: A Framework for Policy*. London, England: SCAA, 1996.

Tower Hamlets Education. *Language Policy*. Tower Hamlets, London, England: Tower Hamlets Education.

Chapter 3: Students

Alberta Education. *ESL Instruction in the Elementary School: Curricular Guidelines and Suggestions*. Edmonton, Alta.: Alberta Education, 1987.

Alberta Education. *English as a Second Language: Elementary Guide to Implementation*. Edmonton, Alta.: Alberta Education, 1996.

Arizona State Board of Education. Rule R7-2-306.

Barking and Dagenham Language Support Service. *Information on Bilingual Children*. Barking, Essex: Language Support Centre.

Burton, S. "Assessment Instruments in the K-12 Independent School System: Finding the Balance between Proficiency and Appropriate TESOL Support." In *Language and Literacy: Finding the Balance*. Proceedings of the ACTA-ATESOL New South Wales National Conference. Leichhardt, NSW: ATESOL NSW, 1995.

Berube, B. *Strategies for Accommodating Limited English Proficient Students*. Augusta, Me.: Maine Department of Education, 1998.

BW Associates. *Meeting the Challenge of Language Diversity: An Evaluation of Programs for Pupils with Limited Proficiency in English. Vol. I—Executive Summary*. Berkeley, Calif.: BW Associates, 1992.

BW Associates. *Meeting the Challenge of Language Diversity. Vol. V—An Exploratory Study of Secondary LEP Programs*. Berkeley, Calif.: BW Associates, 1992.

Catholic Education Office. *English as a Second Language in Catholic Schools K-12: Position Statement*. Sydney, NSW: Catholic Education Office, 1992.

Catholic Education Office. *Successful ESL: Guidelines for Teachers with Newly Arrived and Other Second Language Learners.* Sydney, NSW: Catholic Education Office, 1995.

Clements, S. "January Refugee Survey." *Redbridge Schools' Refugee Newsletter.* Redbridge, Essex: Redbridge Local Education Authority, 1995.

Collier, V.P. "How Long? A Synthesis of Research on Academic Achievement in a Second Language." In *TESOL Quarterly.* Vol. 23, no. 3: September 1989.

Collier, V.C. *Promoting Academic Success for ESL Students.* Elizabeth, N.J.: New Jersey TESOL, 1995.

Commonwealth of Massachusetts Department of Education. *Educating Language Minority Students: Laws, Regulations, Policies and Guidelines in the Commonwealth of Massachusetts.* Quincy, Mass.: Bureau of Equity and Language Services, 1992.

Commonwealth of Pennsylvania Department of Education. *Instructional Support for Students Who Are Culturally and Linguistically Diverse: A Collection of Background Information and Training Materials.* Philadelphia, Pa.: Pennsylvania Department of Education, 1997.

DeBoard, R. & M. Donlin. *Middle School/Bilingual Intervention Team Program: End of Year Report for 1991-1992.* Seattle, Wash.: Seattle Public Schools, Department of Transitional Bilingual Education, c. 1992.

Directorate of School Education, Victoria, Australia. *Education News.* Feb. 10, 1994.

East Sussex County Council. *Bilingual Support Service Handbook: Supporting Bilingual Pupils.* Brighton, Sussex: Bilingual Support Service, 1992.

Faltis, C. & S. Hudelson. "Learning English as an Additional Language in K-12 Schools." In *TESOL Quarterly.* Vol. 28, no. 3: 1994.

Georgia Department of Education. *Georgia ESOL Resource Guide.* Atlanta, Ga.: Georgia Department of Education, c. 1993.

Georgia Department of Education. *English to Speakers of Other Languages Resource Guide.* Atlanta, Ga.: Georgia Department of Education, c. 1995.

Gunderson, L. "Some Findings about School-Age Immigrants in Vancouver." Vancouver, B.C.: University of British Columbia, 1997.

Hamayan, E.V. & R. Perlman. "Helping Language Minority Students after They Exit from Bilingual/ESL Programs." In *Notes for ESL: The Newsletter of the ESL PSA of the B.C.Teachers' Federation.* Vol. 9, no. 1: 1998.

Hertfordshire County Council Education Department. *Assessment of Minority Ethnic Pupils.* Hertford, Hertfordshire: Hertfordshire Education Department, 1997.

Iowa Department of Education. *Educating Iowa's Limited English Proficient Students.* Des Moines, Iowa: Iowa Department of Education, 1996.

Kauffman, D. et al. *Content-ESL across the U.S.A.: Volume II—A Practical Guide.* Washington, D.C.: Center for Applied Linguistics, c. 1995.

Liverpool Bilingual Development Service and Consultancy. "Guidance on Meeting the Needs of Newly Arrived Bilingual Learners in the Early Years." Liverpool, Lancashire: Bilingual Development Service and Consultancy.

Los Angeles Unified School District. "Using Spanish LAS Test Result for Secondary Program Placement. Memorandum 36, June 29." Los Angeles, Calif.: Los Angeles Unified School District, 1993.

Manitoba Education and Training. *Planning for Success: Developing English as a Second Language Protocol.* Winnipeg, Man.: Manitoba Education and Training, 1998.

Maryland State Department of Education. *Better English as a Second Language.* Baltimore, Md.: Maryland State Department of Education, 1991.

Moncton School District Number 2. *The ESL Teachers' Handbook.* Moncton, N.B.: School District No. 2.

North York Board of Education. *Multilingual Education in North York Schools.* North York, Ont.: North York Board of Education, 1996.

Nova Scotia Department of Education. *ESL Resource Document for Teachers/Support Staff.* Halifax, N.S.: Nova Scotia Department of Education, 1994.

Office of Language Minority Programs, School District of Philadelphia. *Guidelines for ESOL/Bilingual Services to Language Minority Students: A Handbook for Schools with ESOL/Bilingual Education Programs.* Philadelphia, Pa.: School District of Philadelphia, 1992.

Office of the Secretary, United States Department of Education. *The Condition of Bilingual Education in the Nation: A Report to the Congress and the President.* Washington, D.C.: United States Department of Education, 1992.

Ohio Department of Education. *Guide to Process and Instruments for Assessing Limited English Proficient Students.* Columbus, Ohio: Ohio Department of Education, 1993.

Ontario Ministry of Education. *English as a Second Language and English Skills Development: Curriculum Guideline — Intermediate and Senior Divisions.* Toronto, Ont.: Ontario Ministry of Education, 1988.

Ontario Ministry of Education and Training. *The Common Curriculum: Policies and Outcomes, Grades 1-9.* Toronto, Ont.: Ontario Ministry of Education and Training, 1995.

Peel Region Board of Education. *Collaboration and Learning.* Mississauga, Ont.: Peel Region Board of Education, c. 1992.

Portland Public Schools. *Bilingual Education Models and Approaches: Theory, Frameworks and Practice.* Portland, Ore.: Portland Public Schools, 1993.

Queensland Education. *Cultural and Language Diversity in Education: Policy and Information Sheets.* Brisbane, Qld.: Education Queensland, 1998.

Saville-Troike, M. "Teaching and Testing for Academic Achievement: The Role of Language Development." In *Occasional Papers in Bilingual Education, Number 4.* Washington, D.C.: National Clearinghouse for Bilingual Education, 1991.

Scarborough Board of Education. *Elementary Guide Grades K-8. Part I: Program Handbook.* Scarborough, Ont.: Scarborough Board of Education, 1988.

Scarborough Board of Education. *Secondary Guide Part I: Program Handbook.* Scarborough, Ont.: Scarborough Board of Education, 1990.

South, H. *OFSTED Report: The Assessment of the Language Development of Bilingual Pupils—A Discussion Paper for NALDIC.* Watford, Hertfordshire: NALDIC, 1997.

State Education Department, University of the State of New York. *Guidelines for Programs under Part 154 of Commissioner's Regulations for Pupils with Limited English Proficiency.* Albany, N.Y.: State Education Department, 1990.

Teachers of English to Speakers of Other Languages. *ESL Standards for PreK-12 Students.* Alexandria, Va.: TESOL, 1997.

Texas Education Agency. "Subchapter A: A State Plan for Educating Limited English Proficient Students." In *Texas Administrative Code and Statutory Citations. Title 19, Part II, #89.5.* Austin, Tex.: Texas Education Agency, 1990.

Vermont Department of Education, Superintendent of Schools. "Memorandum." South Burlington, Vt.: Vermont Department of Education, 1991.

Western Australia Ministry of Education. *Social Justice in Education: Policy and Guidelines for the Education of Non-English-Speaking Background Students.* Perth, WA: Western Australia Ministry of Education, 1991.

Chapter 4: Teachers

Alberta Education. *ESL Instruction in the Elementary School: Curricular Guidelines and Suggestions.* Edmonton, Alta.: Alberta Education, 1987.

Alberta Education. *ESL Instruction in the Junior High School: Curricular Guidelines and Suggestions.* Edmonton, Alta.: Alberta Education, 1988.

Alberta Education. *Elementary English as a Second Language: Guide to Implementation.* Edmonton, Alta.: Alberta Education, 1996.

Allen, H.B. "What It Means to Be a Professional in TESOL." In *IDIOMatically Speaking: Selected Articles from IDIOM, Volumes 1-10.* (J. McConochie, E. Block, G. Brookes & B. Gonzales, Eds.). New York, N.Y.: NYS BEA, 1981.

Altick, S. & M. Kupetz. "State Certification in ESL: Grassroots Efforts Yielding Results." In *TESOL Matters.* Vol. 3, no. 6: December-January, 1993-94.

Ashworth, M. *The First Step on the Longer Path: Becoming an ESL Teacher*. Scarborough, Ont.: Pippin Publishing, 1992.

Ashworth, M. & H.P. Wakefield. *Teaching the World's Children: ESL for Ages Three to Seven*. Scarborough, Ont.: Pippin Publishing, 1994.

Australian Council of TESOL Associations. *The Education of Students from Non-English-Speaking Backgrounds*. Darwin, NT: ACTA, c. 1994.

Barking and Dagenham Language Support Service. *Language Support Service: Bilingual Children in Schools*. Barking, Essex: Barking and Dagenham Local Education Authority.

Bourne, J. *Moving into the Mainstream: LEA Provision for Bilingual Pupils*. Windsor, England: NFER-Nelson, 1989 (Quoted in C. Franson, "The Role of the English as a Second/Additional Language Support Teacher: Necessary Conditions for a New Definition." In *NALDIC Occasional Paper 3*. Watford, Hertfordshire: NALDIC, 1995).

Brent Language Service. *"The Difference between Partnership and Support Teaching*. Brent, London: Brent Language Service, 1992.

Burgess, L.W. "Letters to New ESL Teachers." In *Practical Practices for ESL Teachers*. Augusta, Me.: Maine Department of Education, 1991.

California Department of Education. *Bilingual Education Handbook: Designing Instruction for LEP Students*. Sacramento, Calif.: California Department of Education, 1990.

Chandler, C. "English as a Second Language (ESL): An Update." Report presented to the Halifax District School Board, N.S., 1993.

Christopher, V. "TESOL Professional Certification: Another Look." In *TESOL Matters*. Vol. 4, no. 6: December-January, 1994-95.

Colman, J. "English Language Teacher Training." In *ATESOL Newsletter*. Vol. 20, no. 3: August, 1994.

Commonwealth of Massachusetts Department of Education. *Educating Language Minority Students*. Quincy, Mass.: Massachusetts Department of Education, 1992.

Department of Education and Science, England. *What Is Partnership Teaching?* London, England: HMSO.

Diaz-Rico, L. "The Role of Teacher Educators in Language Policy and Planning." In *TESOL Matters*. Vol. 5, no. 2: April-May, 1995.

Freeman, D. & J.C. Richards. "Conceptions of Teaching and the Education of Second Language Teachers." In *TESOL Quarterly*. Vol. 27, no. 2: 1993.

Guadarrama, I. & B. Leone. "The Evolving Roles of Bilingual/ESL Teachers: New Roles in the Context of Educational Reform." In *TESOL Matters*. Part 1, December-January, 1994-95; Part 2, February-March, 1995.

Harrold, D.K. "Accreditation/Certification for Adult ESL Instructors in Canada: An Overview." In *TESL Canada Journal*. Vol. 13, no. 1: Winter, 1995.

Hogan, S. *TESOL Teacher Competencies Document*. Leichhardt, NSW: ATESOL, 1994.

Home Office, England. "Role of S11 Staff." (Quoted in *Language and Literacy Development for Speakers of English as a Second Language and for Pupils of Afro-Caribbean Origin, Ages 3-11*. Project One. Wolverhampton, England: Wolverhampton Borough Council Education Department, 1991).

Illinois State Board of Education. "Title 23: Education and Cultural Resources—Subchapter f: Section 228.40 (c)." Chicago, Ill.: Illinois State Board of Education, 1992.

Leone, B. & B. Gerner de Garcia. "Can Bilingual and ESL Teachers Also Be Multicultural Teachers?" In *TESOL Matters*. Vol. 5, no. 5: October-November, 1996.

Liverpool Education Directorate. *Language Survey Report*. Liverpool, England: Liverpool Education Directorate, 1995.

Los Angeles Unified School District. "Secondary ESL Academy—Background and Purpose." In *Memorandum 23*. Los Angeles, Calif.: Los Angeles Unified School District, 1993.

Maine Department of Education. *Practical Practices for ESL Teachers*. Augusta, Me.: Maine Department of Education, 1991.

Morley, J. "The Challenges and Rewards of Being an ESOL Professional." In *TESOL Matters*. Vol. 3, no. 6: December-January, 1993-94.

National Association for Language Development in the Curriculum. "Guidance on OFSTED Inspections: Pupils for

Whom English Is an Additional Language." In *NALDIC Working Paper 2*. Watford, Hertfordshire: NALDIC, 1997.

Ohio Department of Education. *Effective Schooling for Language Minority Students: Research and Practices Related to the Establishment and Maintenance of Effective Bilingual Education Programs.* Columbus, Ohio: Ohio Department of Education, 1993.

Peel Region Board of Education. *Collaboration and Learning.* Mississauga, Ont.: Peel Region Board of Education, 1992.

Redbridge Language Support Service. *Handbook.* Ilford, Essex: Redbridge Language Support Service, 1989.

Rubrecht, P. "ESL Accreditation Moves Ahead in Saskatchewan." In *Literacy Works.* Vol. 8, no. 2: 1996-97.

Santiago, R.L. "Academic Success for LEP Students in American Schools: Putting Education Back in Bilingual Education." In *Effective Schooling for Language Minority Students: Research and Practices Related to the Establishment and Maintenance of Effective Bilingual Education Programs.* Columbus, Ohio: Ohio Department of Education, 1993.

Chapter 5: Programs

Alberta Education. *Elementary English as a Second Language: Guide to Implementation.* Edmonton, Alta.: Alberta Education, 1996.

Ashworth, N.M. *Blessed with Bilingual Brains: Education of Immigrant Children with English as a Second Language.* Vancouver, B.C.: Pacific Educational Press, 1988.

Bilingual Education Office, California State Department of Education. *Beyond Language: Social and Cultural Factors in Schooling Language Minority Students.* Los Angeles, Calif.: California State University, 1986.

BW Associates. *Meeting the Challenge of Language Diversity: An Evaluation of Programs for Pupils with Limited Proficiency in English. Vol. 2. Findings and Conclusions.* Berkeley, Calif.: BW Associates, 1992.

Commonwealth of Pennsylvania Department of Education. *Instructional Support for Students Who are Culturally and Linguistically Diverse: A Collection of Background Information and*

Training Materials. Philadelphia, Pa.: Pennsylvania Department of Education, 1997.

Esling, J.H., Ed. *Multicultural Education and Policy in the 1990s*. Toronto, Ont.: OISE Press, 1989.

Genesse, F. *Educating Second Language Children: The Whole Child, the Whole Curriculum, the Whole Community*. New York, N.Y.: Cambridge University Press, 1994.

Manitoba Education and Training. *Planning for Success: Developing an English as a Second Language Protocol: A Resource for Kindergarten to Senior 4 Schools*. Winnipeg, Man.: Manitoba Education and Training, 1998.

Minnesota Department of Children, Families and Learning. *Guidelines for Serving Students with Limited English Proficiency: Administrative Manual*. St. Paul, Minn.: Minnesota Department of Children, Families and Learning, 1998.

National Association for Language Development in the Curriculum. *Bilingual Pupils Learning English as an Additional Language: Guidelines for Classroom and School Practices: NALDIC Working Paper 1*. Watford, Hertfordshire: NALDIC, 1997.

National Association for Language Development in the Curriculum. *Guidelines on Bilingualism: NALDIC Working Paper 3*. Watford, Hertfordshire: NALDIC, 1998.

Peel Region Board of Education. *ESL/ESD Program Review*. Mississauga, Ont.: Peel Region Board of Education, 1996.

Peel Region Board of Education. *ESL/ESD Program Review: Supplementary Research Information*. Mississauga, Ont.: Peel Region Board of Education, 1996.

Queensland Department of Education. *Cultural and Language Diversity in Education. Book 1—A Whole School Approach; Book 2—Texts for Children; Book 3—Overcoming Barriers for Parents; Policy and Information Sheets*. Brisbane, Qld.: Queensland Department of Education, 1998.

Scarborough Board of Education. *ESL/ESD Handbook for Elementary Programs*. Scarborough, Ont.: Scarborough Board of Education, 1988.

South Australian Education Department. *Review of the English as a Second Language Program*. Adelaide, SA: South Australian Education Department, 1987.

Victoria Department of School Education. *English as a Second Language (ESL) in Government Schools.* Melbourne, Vic.: Directorate of School Education, 1992.

Chapter 6: Bilingual Education

Arizona Department of Education. *Bilingual Programs and English as a Second Language Programs: School Year 1996-97 Report.* Phoenix, Ariz.: Arizona Department of Education, 1998.

BW Associates. *Meeting the Challenge of Language Diversity: An Evaluation of Programs for Pupils with Limited Proficiency in English.* Berkeley, Calif.: BW Associates, 1992.

California Department of Education. *Bilingual Education Handbook: Designing Instruction for LEP Students.* Sacramento, Calif.: California Department of Education, 1990.

Chamot, A.U. "TESOL Testifies on the U.S. Language Fluency Act." In *TESOL Matters.* Vol. 8, no. 5: August-September, 1998.

Christian, D. & C. Mahrer. *Two-Way Bilingual Programs in the United States, 1991-1992.* Washington, D.C.: National Center for Research on Cultural Diversity and Second Language Learning, 1992.

Connecticut State Board of Education. *Position Statements.* Hartford, Conn.: Connecticut State Board of Education, 1997.

Crawford, J. *Hold Your Tongue: Bilingualism and the Politics of "English Only."* New York, N.Y.: Addison Wesley, 1992.

Cummins, J. & M. Danesi. *Heritage Languages: The Development and Denial of Canada's Linguistic Resources.* Montreal, Que.: La Maitresse d'école, 1990.

Genesee, F. *Learning through Two Languages: Studies of Immersion and Bilingual Education.* Cambridge, Mass.: Newbury House, 1987.

Greenwich Directorate of Education. "Bilingualism and Community Languages." London Borough of Greenwich: Directorate of Education.

Hertfordshire County Council. *Assessment of Competence in the First/Home Language.* Hertford, Hertfordshire: Hertfordshire County Council, 1996.

Imhoff, G., Ed. *Learning in Two Languages: From Conflict to Consensus in the Reorganization of Schools.* New Brunswick, N.J.: Transaction, 1990.

Iowa Department of Education. *Educating Iowa's Limited English Proficient Students.* Des Moines, Iowa: Iowa Department of Education, 1996.

Krashen, S.D. *Bilingual Education: A Focus on Current Research.* Washington, D.C.: National Clearinghouse for Bilingual Education, 1991.

National Association for Language Development in the Curriculum. *Guidelines on Bilingualism. NALDIC Working Paper 3.* Watford, Hertfordshire: NALDIC, 1998.

National Association for Language Development in the Curriculum. *Guidelines on Baseline Assessment for Bilingual Children. NALDIC Working Paper 4.* Watford, Hertfordshire: NALDIC, 1998.

Padilla, A.M, H.H. Fairchild & C.M. Valdez, Eds. *Bilingual Education: Issues and Strategies.* Newbury Park, Calif.: Sage Publications, 1990.

Portland Public Schools. *Bilingual Education Models and Approaches: Theory, Frameworks and Practice.* Portland, Ore.: Portland Public Schools, 1993.

Redbridge Language Support Service. *Redbridge Language Support Service Handbook.* London, England: Redbridge Language Support Service, 1989.

TESOL. *TESOL Statement on the Role of Bilingual Education in the Education of Children in the United States.* Alexandria, Va.: TESOL, 1992.

TESOL. *ESL Standards for Pre-K-12 Students.* Alexandria, Va.: TESOL, 1997.

Texas Education Agency. *Texas Education Code: Commissioner's Rules Concerning Limited English Proficient Students— #89.1210 Program Content and Design.* Austin, Tex.: Texas Education Agency, 1996.

Unz, R.K. & G.M. Tuchman. "One Homogeneous Nation— The Unz Initiative." In *Proposition 227.* California, 1997.

Chapter 7: Curriculum and Methods

Alberta Education. *Elementary English as a Second Language: Guide to Implementation.* Edmonton, Alta.: Alberta Education, 1996.

Ashworth, N.M. 1995. "Teaching Language and Content in Canada, the United States, and England." In *TESL Manitoba Journal.* Vol. 10, no. 4: 1995.

Australian Education Council. *ESL Scales.* Carlton, Vic.: Curriculum Corporation, 1994.

British Columbia Ministry of Education. *ESL Resource Book: Volume I—Integrating Language and Content Instruction K-12.* Victoria, B.C.: B.C. Ministry of Education, 1986.

Burkart, G. *Content-ESL across the U.S.A.: A Training Packet. Volume III.* Washington, D.C.: Center for Applied Linguistics, 1994.

Campbell, B. & C. Halsall. *Lessons in Literacy: Case Studies of Successful Strategies for Raising Achievement in Multilingual Schools.* Bradford, England: Bradford Education, 1998.

Cazden, C.B. "One Australian High School's Version of 'Language Teaching across the Curriculum.'" In *TESOL Matters.* Vol. 6, no. 3: 1996.

Chamot, A.U. & J.M. O'Malley. *A Cognitive Academic Language Learning Approach: An ESL Content-Based Curriculum.* Wheaton, Md.: National Clearinghouse for Bilingual Education, 1986.

Chamot, A.U. & J.M. O'Malley. "The Cognitive Academic Language Learning Approach: A Bridge to the Mainstream." In *TESOL Quarterly.* Vol. 2, no. 2: 1987.

Chamot, A.U. & J.M. O'Malley. *The CALLA Handbook.* Reading, Mass.: Addison-Wesley, 1994.

Chamot, A.U., J.M. O'Malley & L. Kupper. *Building Bridges: Content and Learning Strategies for ESL Students. Student Books 1, 2 and 3.* Boston, Mass.: Heinle & Heinle, 1992.

Chevalier, M. "Seeking New Paths: Whole Language in ESL and Bilingual Classrooms." In *TESOL Matters.* Vol. 5, no. 1: February-March, 1995.

Citizenship & Immigration Canada. *Canadian Language Benchmarks: English as a Second Language for Adults; English as a Sec-*

ond Language for Literacy Learners. Ottawa, Ont.: Minister of Supply and Services Canada, 1996.

Crandall, J.A. "Content-Centered Learning in the United States." In *Annual Review of Applied Linguistics.* Vol. 13: 1993.

Department for Education, England. *The National Curriculum.* London, England: HMSO, 1995.

Early, M. & G. Tang. "Helping ESL Students Cope with Content-Based Texts." In *TESL Canada Journal.* Vol. 8, no. 2: 1991.

Faltis, C. & S. Hudelson. "Learning English as an Additional Language in K-12 Schools." In *TESOL Quarterly.* Vol. 28, no. 3: 1994.

Genesee, F. *Integrating Language and Content: Lessons from Immersion.* Washington, D.C.: National Center for Research on Cultural Diversity and Second Language Learning, 1994.

Heald-Taylor, G. *Whole Language Strategies for ESL Students.* San Diego, Calif.: Dormac Inc., 1989.

Hindmarsh, M. *Approach to Teaching ESL—Junior High Interactive Learning Approach.* Calgary, Alta.: Calgary Catholic Board of Education, 1990.

Huss, R.L. "Young Children Become Literate in English as a Second Language." In *TESOL Quarterly.* Vol. 29, no. 4: 1995.

Iowa Department of Education. *Educating Iowa's Limited English Proficiency Students.* Des Moines, Iowa: Iowa Department of Education, 1996.

Jacob, E. & B. Mattson. "Cooperative Learning: Instructing Limited-English-Proficient Students in Heterogeneous Classes." In *Bilingual Education: Issues and Strategies.* A.M. Padilla, H.H.Fairchild & C.M. Valdez, Eds. Newbury Park, Calif.: Sage Publications, 1990.

Kauffman, D. *Content-ESL across the U.S.A.: A Practical Guide. Volume II.* Washington, D.C.: Center for Applied Linguistics, 1994.

Kidd, R. & B. Marquardson. *Sourcebook for Integrating ESL and Content Instruction Using the Foresee Approach.* Winnipeg, Man.: Manitoba Education and Training, 1994.

Kidd, R. & B. Marquardson. *Secondary Sourcebook for Integrating ESL and Content Instruction Using the Foresee Approach.* Winnipeg, Man.: Manitoba Education and Training, 1994.

Kidd, R. & B. Marquardson. "The Foresee Approach for ESL Strategy Instruction in an Academic-Proficiency Context." In *Language Learning Strategies around the World: Cross-Cultural Perspectives*. R. Oxford, Ed. Honolulu, Hawaii: University of Hawaii, 1996.

Kidd, R. & B. Marquardson. "The Foresee Approach to Integrated ESL Instruction." In *TESL Canada Journal*. Vol. 15, no. 1: 1997.

Kidd, R. & B. Marquardson. "The Spirit of Foresee." In *TESL Manitoba Journal*. Vol. 12, no. 4: 1997.

Krashen, S. & T. Terrell. *The Natural Approach: Language Acquisition in the Classroom*. Hayward, Calif.: Alemany Press, 1983.

Manitoba Education and Training. *Towards Inclusion: Programming for English as a Second Language Students, Senior 1-4.* Winnipeg, Man.: Manitoba Education and Training, 1996.

Mohan, B. *Language and Content*. Reading, Mass.: Addison-Wesley, 1986.

New Jersey State Department of Education. *Guidelines for Development of Program Plan and Evaluation Summary: Bilingual/ESL Programs and English Language Services.* Trenton, N.J.: New Jersey State Department of Education, 1991.

New York State Education Department. *Guidelines for Programs under Part 154 of Commissioner's Regulations for Pupils with Limited English Proficiency.* Albany, N.Y.: University of the State of New York, New York State Education Department, 1991.

Office of Language Minority Programs, School District of Philadelphia. *Guidelines for ESOL/Bilingual Services to Language Minority Students: A Handbook for Schools with ESOL/Bilingual Education Programs.* Philadelphia, Pa.: School District of Philadelphia, 1992.

Ontario Ministry of Education and Training. *The Common Curriculum: Policies and Outcomes, Grades 1-9.* Toronto, Ont.: Ontario Ministry of Education and Training, 1995.

Ontario Ministry of Education and Training. *The Ontario Curriculum, Grades 1-8: Language.* Toronto, Ont.: Ontario Ministry of Education and Training, 1997.

Richards-Amato, P.A. & M.A. Snow. *Introduction: The Multicultural Classroom—Reading for Content Area Teachers.* London, England: Longmans, 1992.

Richards, J.C. & D. Hurley. "Language and Content: Approaches to Curriculum Alignment." In *The Language Teaching Matrix.* J.C. Richards, Ed. Cambridge, England: Cambridge University Press, 1990.

School Curriculum and Assessment Authority. *Teaching English as an Additional Language.* London, England: School Curriculum and Assessment Authority, 1996.

Sheppard, K. *Content-ESL across the U.S.A.: A Technical Report. Volume I.* Washington, D.C.: Center for Applied Linguistics, 1994.

Short, D.J. *How to Integrate Language and Content Instruction: A Training Manual.* Washington, D.C.: Center for Applied Linguistics, 1991.

Short, D.J. "Assessing Integrated Language and Content Instruction." In *TESOL Quarterly.* Vol. 27, no. 4: 1993.

Short, D.J. "Expanding Middle School Horizons: Integrating Language, Culture and Social Studies." In *TESOL Quarterly.* Vol. 28, no. 3: 1994.

Silvern, L. "Sheltered English." California: Emergency Immigrant Education Assistance Program.

Tang, G.M. "Teaching Collaboration in Integrating Language and Content." In *TESL Canada Journal.* Vol. 11, no. 2: 1994.

Tang, G.M. "Teaching Content Knowledge and ESOL in Multicultural Classrooms." In *TESOL Journal.* Vol. 2, no. 2: 1992-93.

Teemant, A., E. Bernhardt & M. Rodriguez-Munoz. "Collaborating with Content-Area Teachers: What We Need to Share." In *TESOL Journal.* Vol. 5, no. 4: 1996.

Tennessee Department of Education. *English as a Second Language: Curriculum Framework.* Nashville, Tenn.: Tennessee Department of Education, 1997.

Tennessee Department of Education. *English as a Second Language: Resource Guide.* Nashville, Tenn.: Tennessee Department of Education, 1997.

Wong, F.L. "Teaching English through Content: Instructional Reform in Programmes for Language Minority Students." In *Multicultural Education and Policy: ESL in the 1990s.* J. Esling, Ed. Toronto, Ont.: OISE Press, 1989.

Chapter 8: Parents and Communities

Alberta Education. *ESL Instruction in the Elementary School: Curricular Guidelines and Suggestions.* Edmonton, Alta.: Alberta Education, 1987.

Alberta Education. *English as a Second Language (ESL) in Alberta Schools: Parent Handbook.* Edmonton, Alta.: Alberta Education, 1993.

Ashworth, N.M. *Beyond Methodology: Second Language Teaching and the Community.* Cambridge, England: Cambridge University Press, 1985.

Ashworth, N.M., J. Cummins & J. Handscombe. *Report of the External Review Team on the Vancouver School Board's ESL Programs.* Vancouver, B.C.: Vancouver School Board, 1989.

Berube, B. *Strategies for Accommodating Limited English Proficient Students.* Augusta, Me.: Maine Department of Education, 1998.

British Columbia Teachers' Federation. *The Views of Parents of ESL Students concerning the British Columbia Education System.* Vancouver, B.C.: British Columbia Teachers' Federation, 1993.

California State Department of Education. *Bilingual Immersion Education: A Program for the Year 2000 and Beyond.* Working Draft. Sacramento, Calif.: Bilingual Education Office, California Department of Education, 1990.

Fenton, S. "How to Get Parents Out." In *Notes for ESL: The Newsletter of the ESL PSA (Provincial Specialists' Association).* Vancouver, B.C.: British Columbia Teachers' Federation, 1998.

Iowa Department of Education. *Educating Iowa's Limited English Proficient Students: A Handbook for Administrators and Teachers.* Des Moines, Iowa: Iowa Department of Education, 1996.

Minnesota Department of Education. *Guidelines for Serving Students with Limited English Proficiency: Administrative Manual.* St. Paul, Minn.: Minnesota Department of Education, 1998.

Nova Scotia Department of Education. *Administrators' ESL Resource Document.* Halifax, N.S.: Nova Scotia Department of Education, 1994.

Ohio Department of Education. *Effective Schooling for Language Minority Students.* Foreword by Ramon L. Santiago. Columbus, Ohio: Ohio Department of Education, 1993.

Queensland Department of Education. *Social Justice Strategy 1994-1998: Book 2—Issues and Strategies.* Brisbane, Qld.: Queensland Department of Education, 1994.

Queensland Department of Education. *Cultural and Language Diversity in Education: Book 3 — Overcoming Barriers for Parents.* Brisbane, Qld.: Queensland Department of Education, 1998.

Richmond School District. *Review of ESL Support Services.* Richmond, B.C.: Richmond School District, 1995.

Seattle Public Schools. *Department of Transitional Bilingual Ed./Comp. Ed./Even Start Operations Manual.* Seattle, Wash.: Seattle Public Schools, c. 1993-94.

Toronto Board of Education. *Welcome to Toronto Kindergartens.* Toronto, Ont.: Toronto Board of Education, 1994.

Zuniga, C. & S.A. Alva. "Parents as Resources in Schools: A Community-of-Learners Perspective." In *The Journal of Educational Issues of Language Minority Students.* Vol. 16: 1996.

Chapter 9: Looking Ahead

Ashworth, N.M. "Projecting the Past into the Future: A Look at ESL for Children in Canada." In *Beyond Multicultural Education: International Perspectives.* Kogila A. Moodley, Ed. Calgary, Alta.: Detselig Enterprises, 1992.

Ashworth, N.M. "Views and Visions." In *Socio-Political Aspects of ESL.* B. Burnaby & A. Cumming, Eds. Toronto, Ont.: OISE Press, 1992.

Banks, J.A. "A Curriculum for Empowerment, Action and Change." In *Beyond Multicultural Education: International Per-*

spectives. Kogila A. Moodley, Ed. Calgary, Alta.: Detselig Enterprises, 1992.

Cummins, J. "Concluding Remarks: Language for Empowerment." In *Minority Education: From Shame to Struggle.* T. Skutnabb-Kangas & J. Cummins, Eds. Philadelphia, Pa.: Multilingual Matters, 1988.

Handscombe, J. "Mainstreaming: Who Needs It?" In *Multicultural Education and Policy: ESL in the 1990s.* J.H. Esling, Ed. Toronto, Ont.: OISE Press, 1989.

Naisbitt, J. & P. Aburdene, P. *Megatrends 2000: Ten New Directions for the 1990s.* New York, N.Y.: William Morrow, 1990.

Toohey, K. "We Teach English as a Second Language to Bilingual Students." In *Socio-Political Aspects of ESL.* B. Burnaby & A. Cumming, Eds. Toronto, Ont.: OISE Press, 1992.

Wittenberg, A.I. *The Prime Imperatives: Priorities in Education.* Toronto, Ont.: Clarke Irwin, 1968.